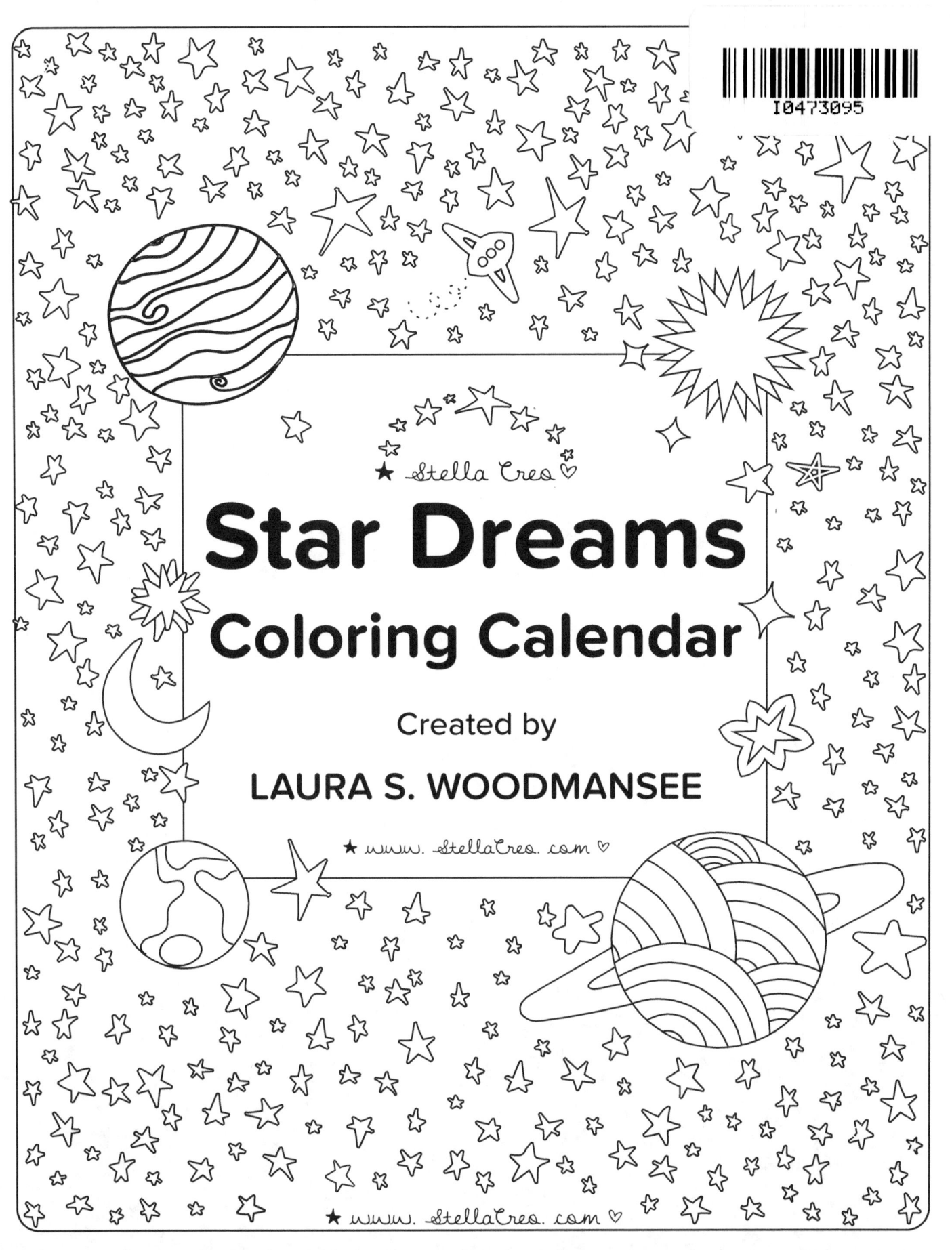

★ Stella Cres ♡

Star Dreams
Coloring Calendar

Created by

LAURA S. WOODMANSEE

★ www. StellaCres. com ♡

★ www. StellaCres. com ♡

this book belongs to:

Dedication

For my Readers, Family, & Friends,
thank you for your loving encouragement.
My wish is that you enjoy this little book
and use it to make your dreams come true!

All My Love,
Laura

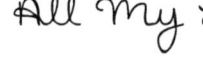

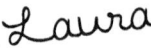

STAR DREAMS

Star Dreams: Deluxe Coloring Calendar

Written & Designed by Laura S. Woodmansee

ISBN-10: 0-9863172-5-X
ISBN-13: 978-0-9863172-5-5

Published in 2015 by Stella Creo inc.
Text and Illustrations © 2015 Stella Creo inc.
Stella Creo inc. and all associated logos are trademarks and/or registered trademarks of Stella Creo inc. www.StellaCreo.com.

Our books are available at special discounts when purchased in quantity for shops, promotions, fundraising, educational use, etc. Contact us via www.StellaCreo.com.

Stella Creo inc. creates STEAM-inspired books, games, and gifts for kids, teens, and grown-ups too.
www.StellaCreo.com

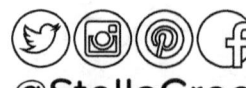
@StellaCreo

★ www. StellaCreo. com ♡

 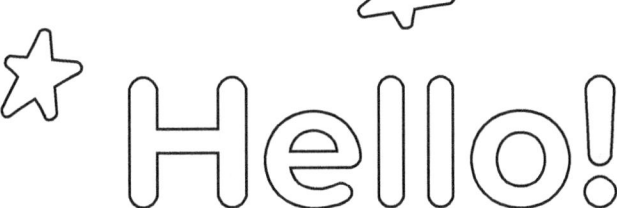  

Hello!

Thanks very much for picking up my new book. I created Star Dreams because I love space, star-filled skies, writing, doodling, and coloring!

This project started out as a space-themed coloring book, but I quickly realized that I wanted my little book to be so much more - a place for dreaming, drawing, and planning. When I told my friends, family, and readers, they were really excited! They encouraged me to share all the different types of coloring pages. So, I combined my star-themed coloring pages with space for notes, doodles, ideas, and dreams. I hope that you enjoy the Star Dreams series as much as I've enjoyed creating it all.

This book has two parts; the Calendars section and the Fun Sheets section. Each has fun, space-themed patterns and designs ready for coloring and creating. The Calendar section has 12 undated star-themed months with matching lined and unlined note pages. The undated calendars can be used with any month and any year. Write in the month at the top and the date in each cute little box. The Fun-Sheets are practical for every day planning, or dreaming about the future. Sheets include; about me, bookmarks, lists, mind maps, project planner, gift lists, gift tags, and more! Photocopy them when you need more.

When we take a few minutes each day to create with color we are happier. So, please pick up a rainbow of crayons or markers and color away. The bright, happy colors on white paper will make you smile.

Please share your colorful pages with us on Instagram, we're @StellaCreo. Tag us with the hash tag #coloringbook. We will share too!

Starry Wishes and Happy Creating,
Laura

P.S.: If you like this book, please check out our other Star Dreams series books. The Star Dreams Deluxe Coloring Journal (ISBN 978-0-9863172-4-8) combines this book and the Star Dreams Coloring Pages (ISBN 978-0-9863172-3-1). www.StellaCreo.com & Amazon.com. Join our e-mail list for free Star Dreams printables and discounts.

@LauraWoodmansee
@StellaCreo

 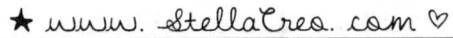

★ www. StellaCreo. com ♡

calendars

Starry Suggestion:

Date your own calendar
Start with any month. Add
your events and special days.
You can also use stickers like the ones
in the **Copy & Use** Section at
the back of the book.

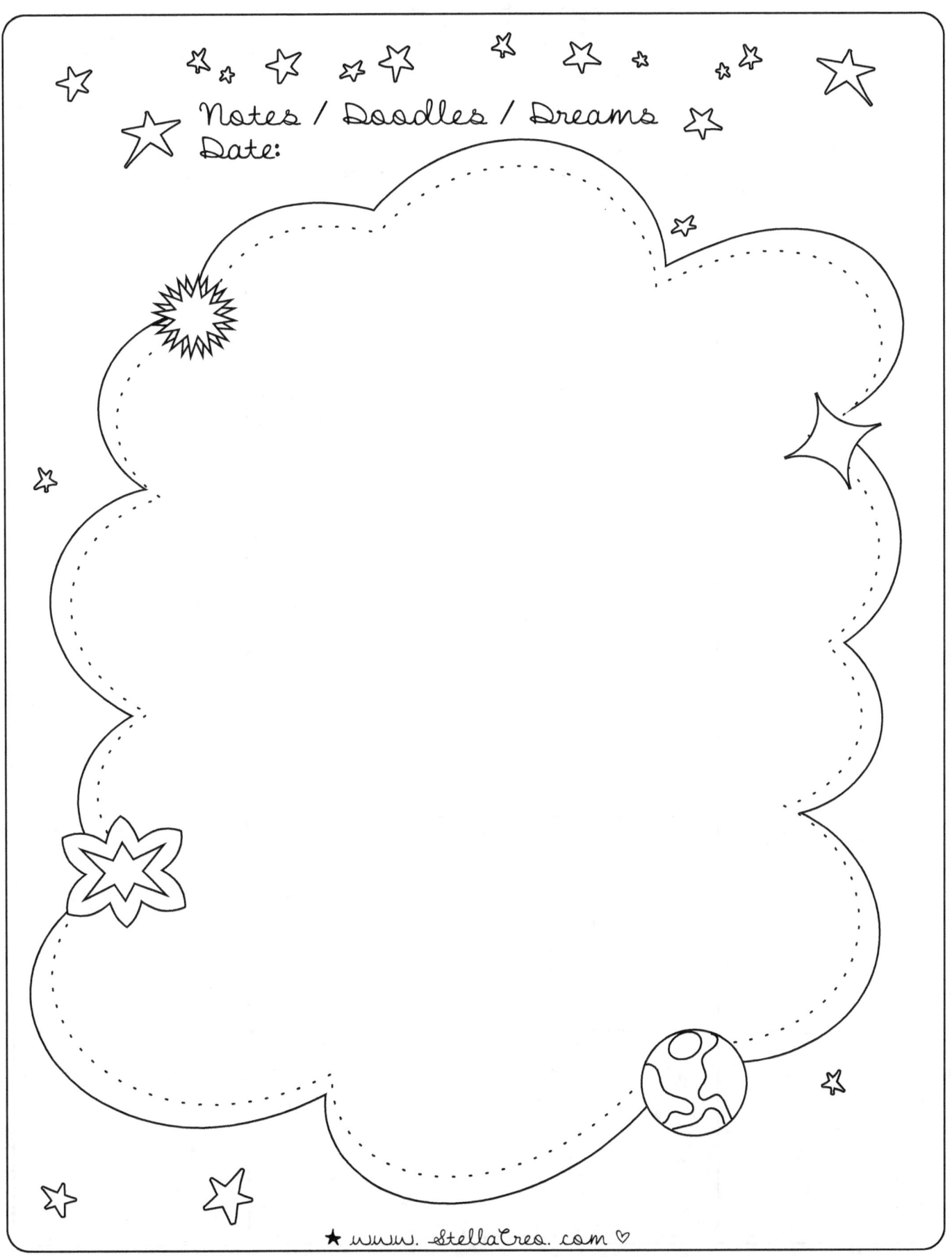

Notes / Doodles / Dreams
Date:

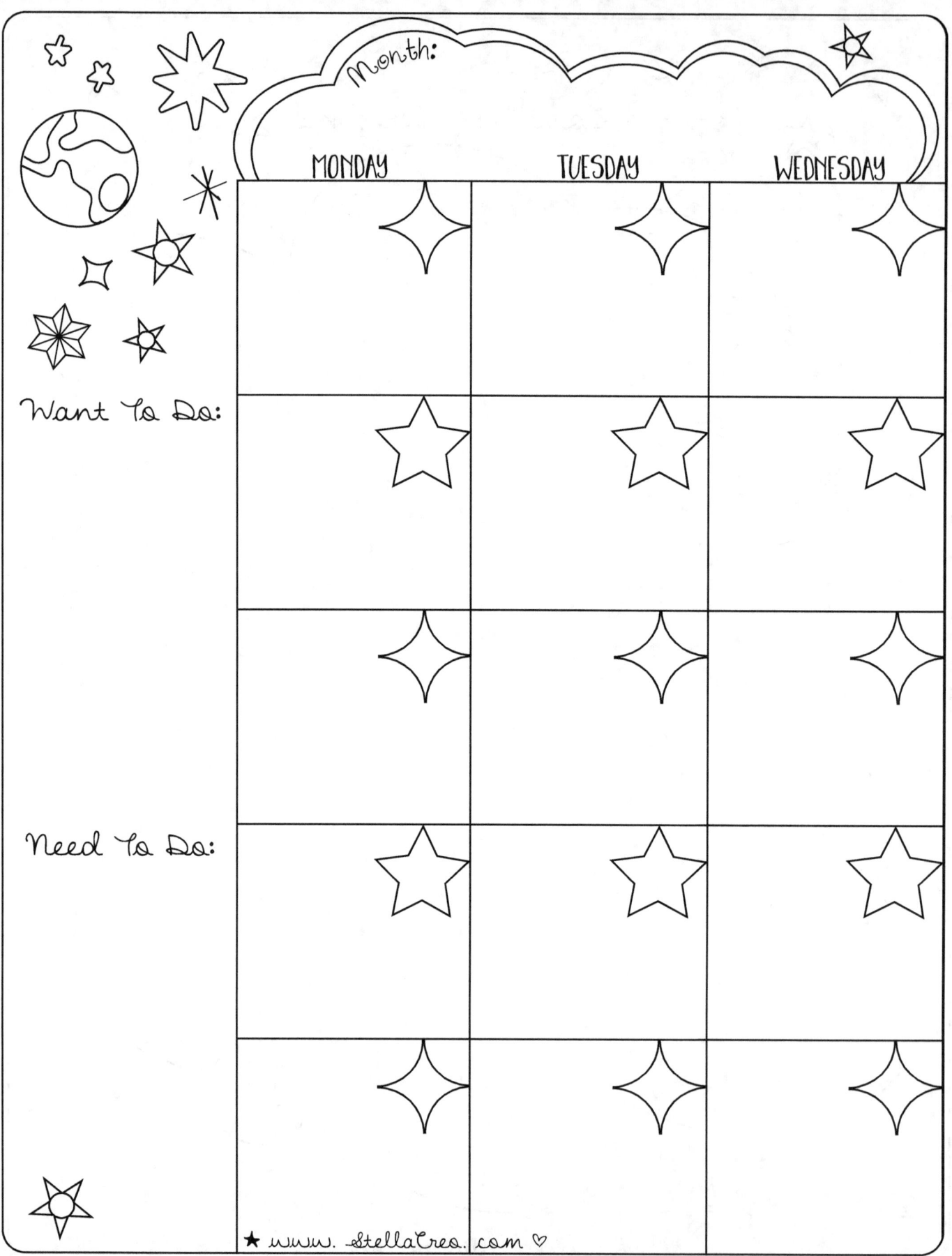

Month:

MONDAY	TUESDAY	WEDNESDAY

Want To Do:

Need To Do:

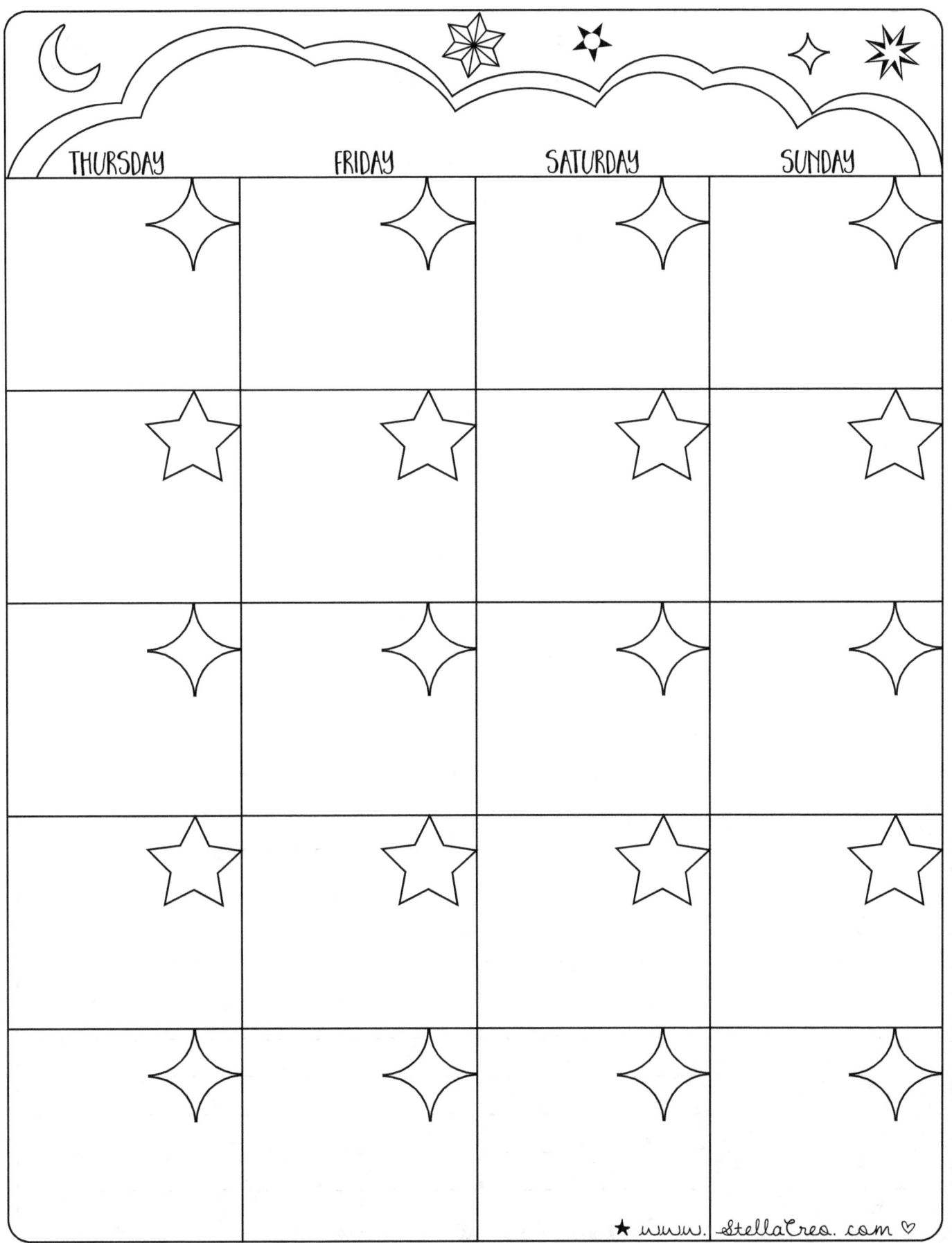

THURSDAY   FRIDAY   SATURDAY   SUNDAY

★ www. stellaCrea. com ♡

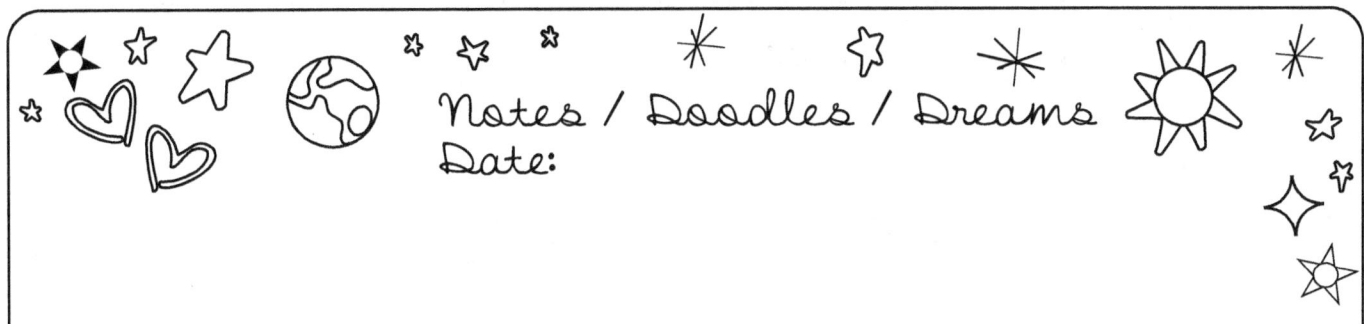

Notes / Doodles / Dreams
Date:

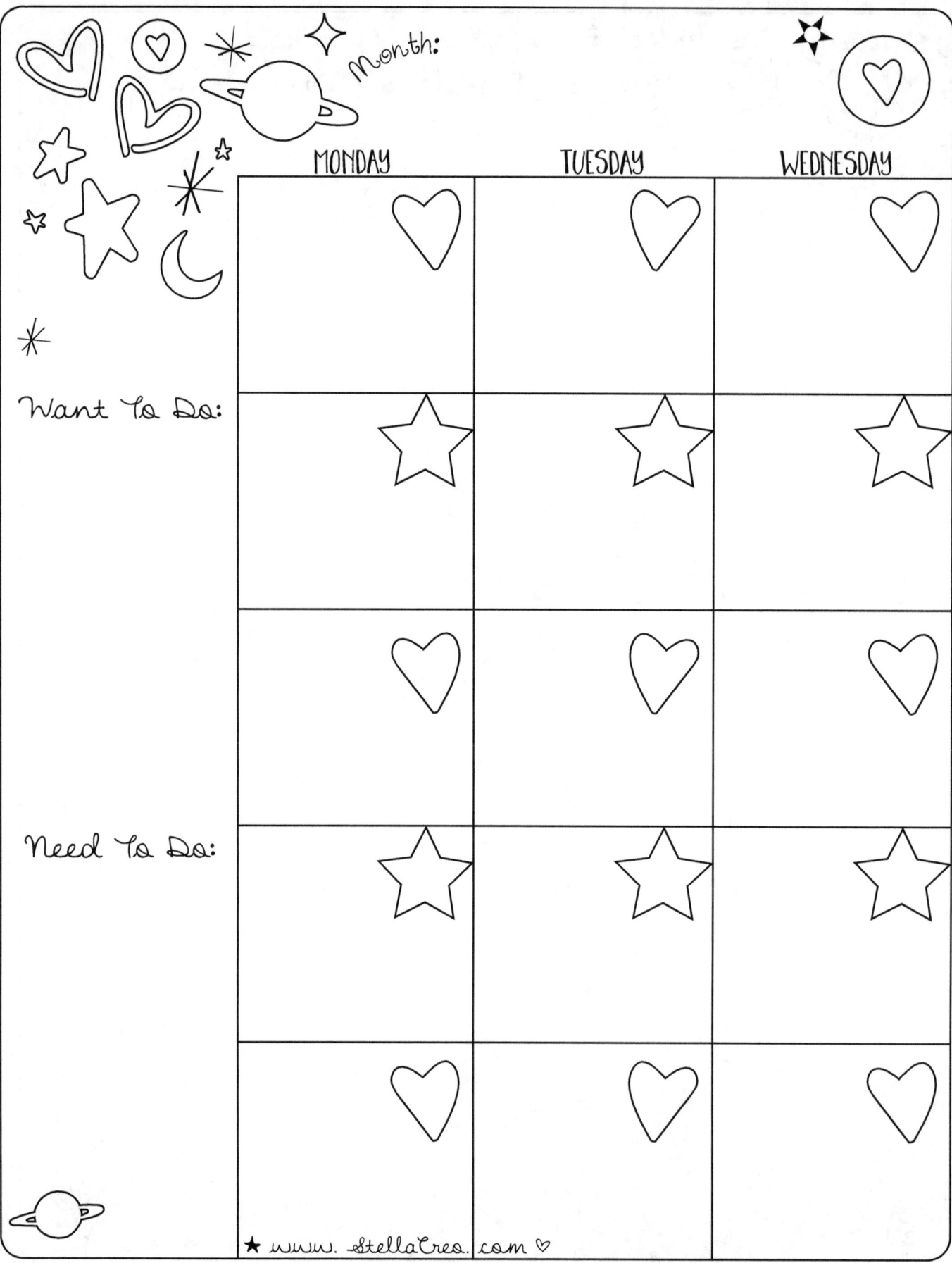

Month:

MONDAY	TUESDAY	WEDNESDAY

Want To Do:

Need To Do:

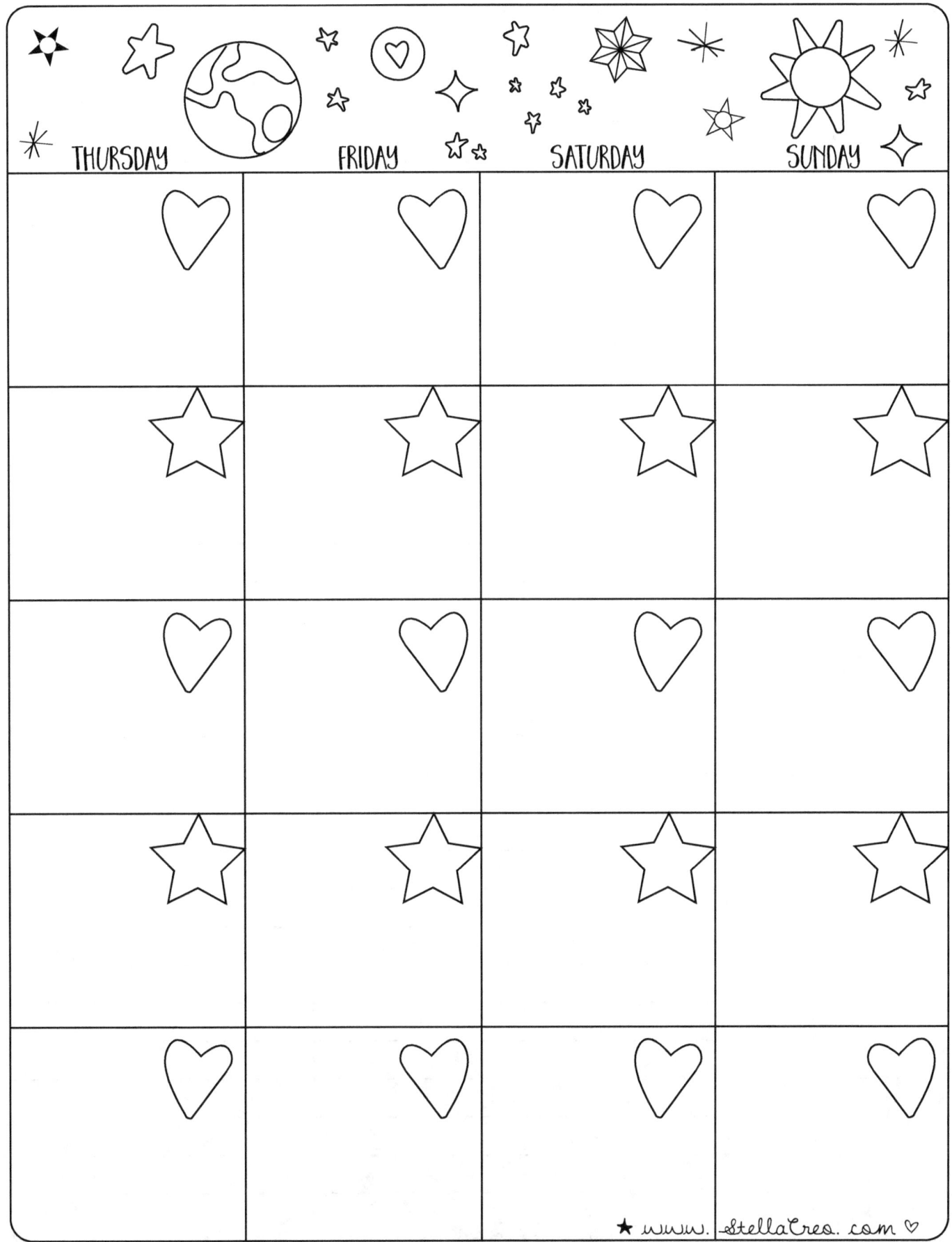

THURSDAY	FRIDAY	SATURDAY	SUNDAY

www. StellaCrea. com

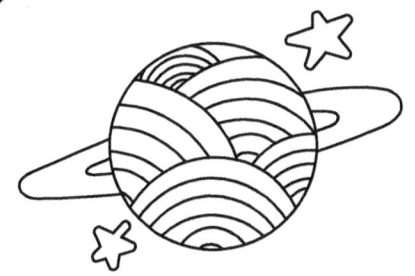

Notes / Doodles / Dreams
Date:

Month:

	MONDAY	TUESDAY	WEDNESDAY
Want To Do:			
Need To Do:			

THURSDAY	FRIDAY	SATURDAY	SUNDAY

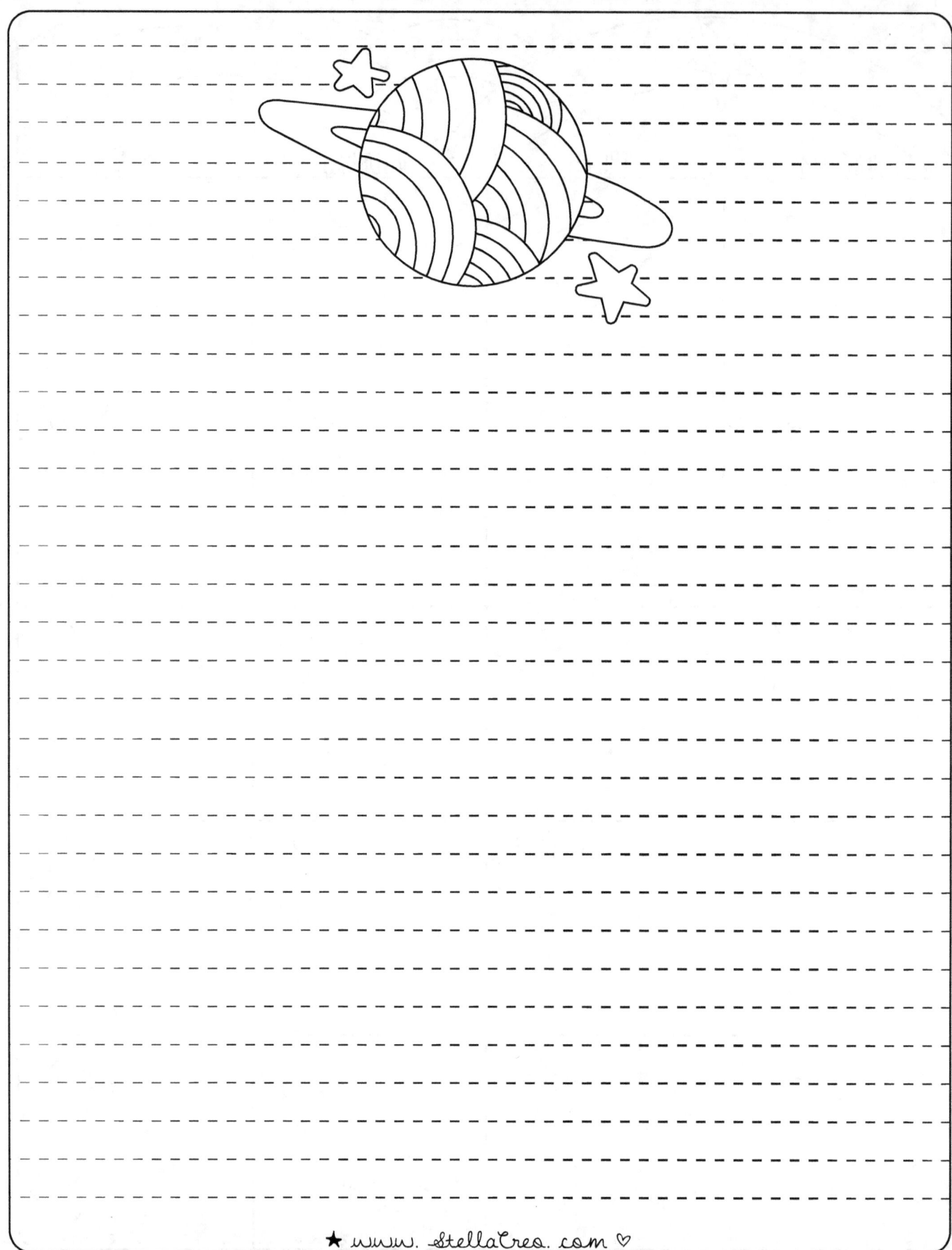

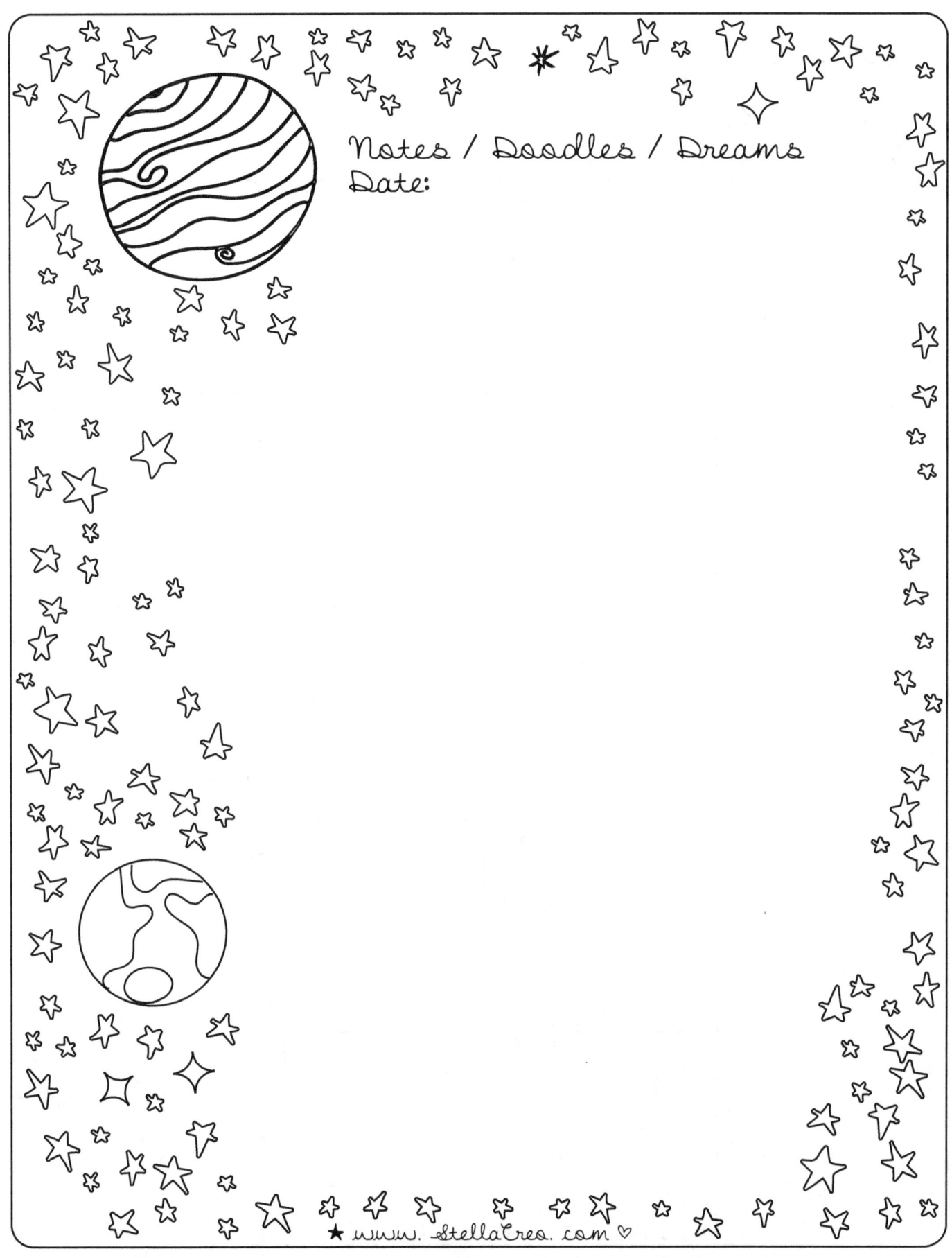

Notes / Doodles / Dreams
Date:

Month:

	MONDAY	TUESDAY	WEDNESDAY
Want To Do:			
Need To Do:			

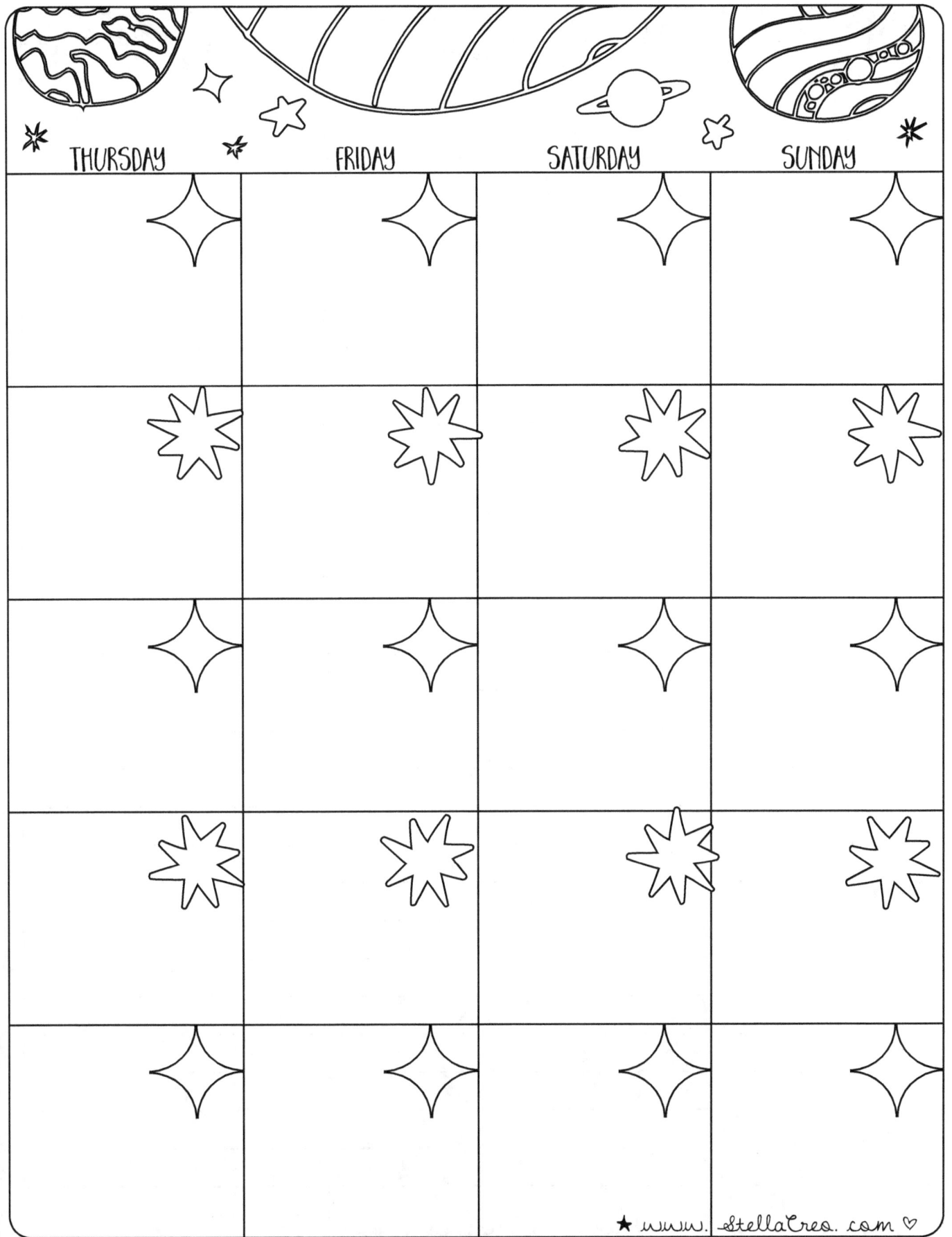

THURSDAY | FRIDAY | SATURDAY | SUNDAY

Notes / Doodles / Dreams
Date:

Month:

	MONDAY	TUESDAY	WEDNESDAY
Want To Do:			
Need To Do:			

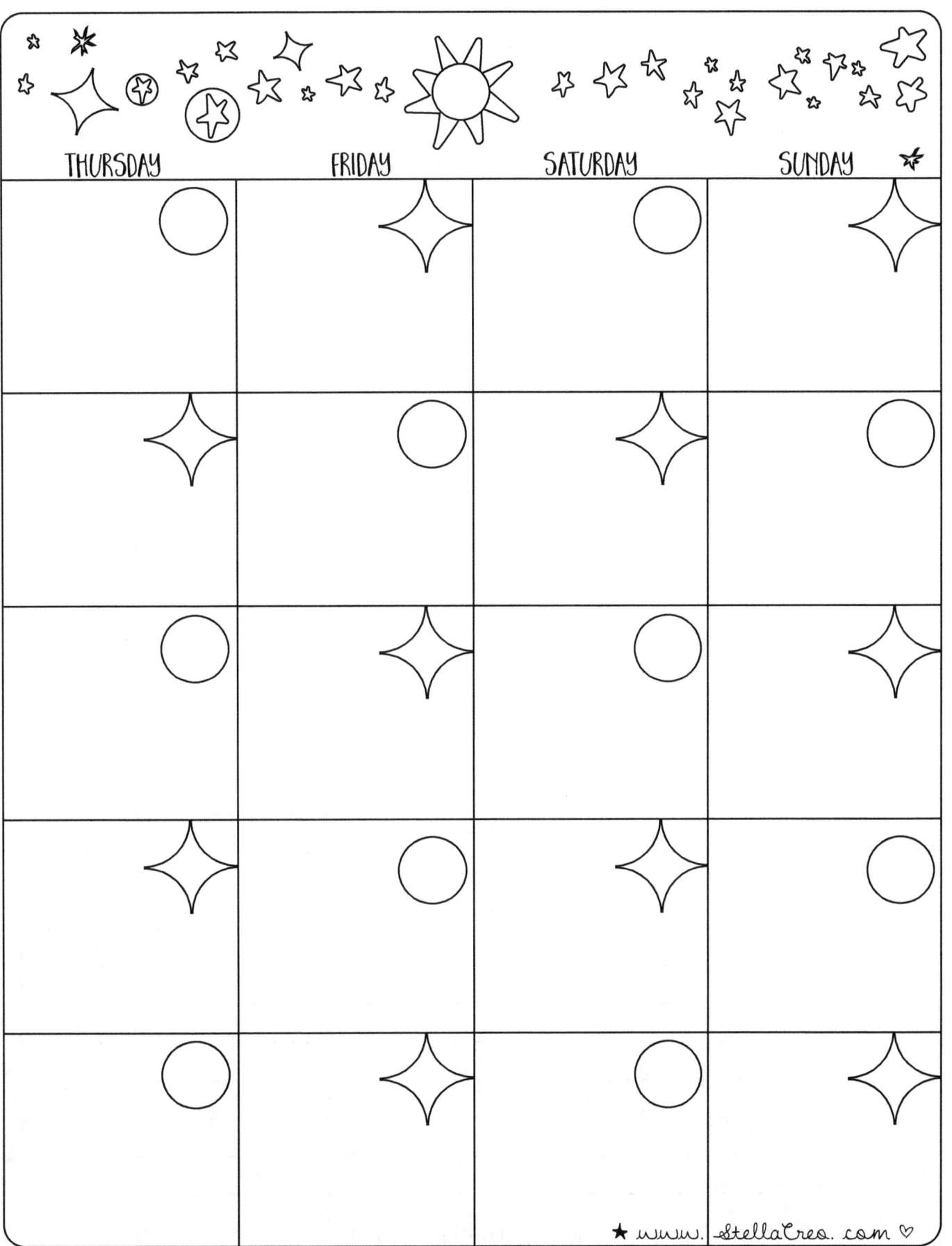

THURSDAY FRIDAY SATURDAY SUNDAY

Notes / Doodles / Dreams
Date:

Month:

MONDAY	TUESDAY	WEDNESDAY

Want To Do:

Need To Do:

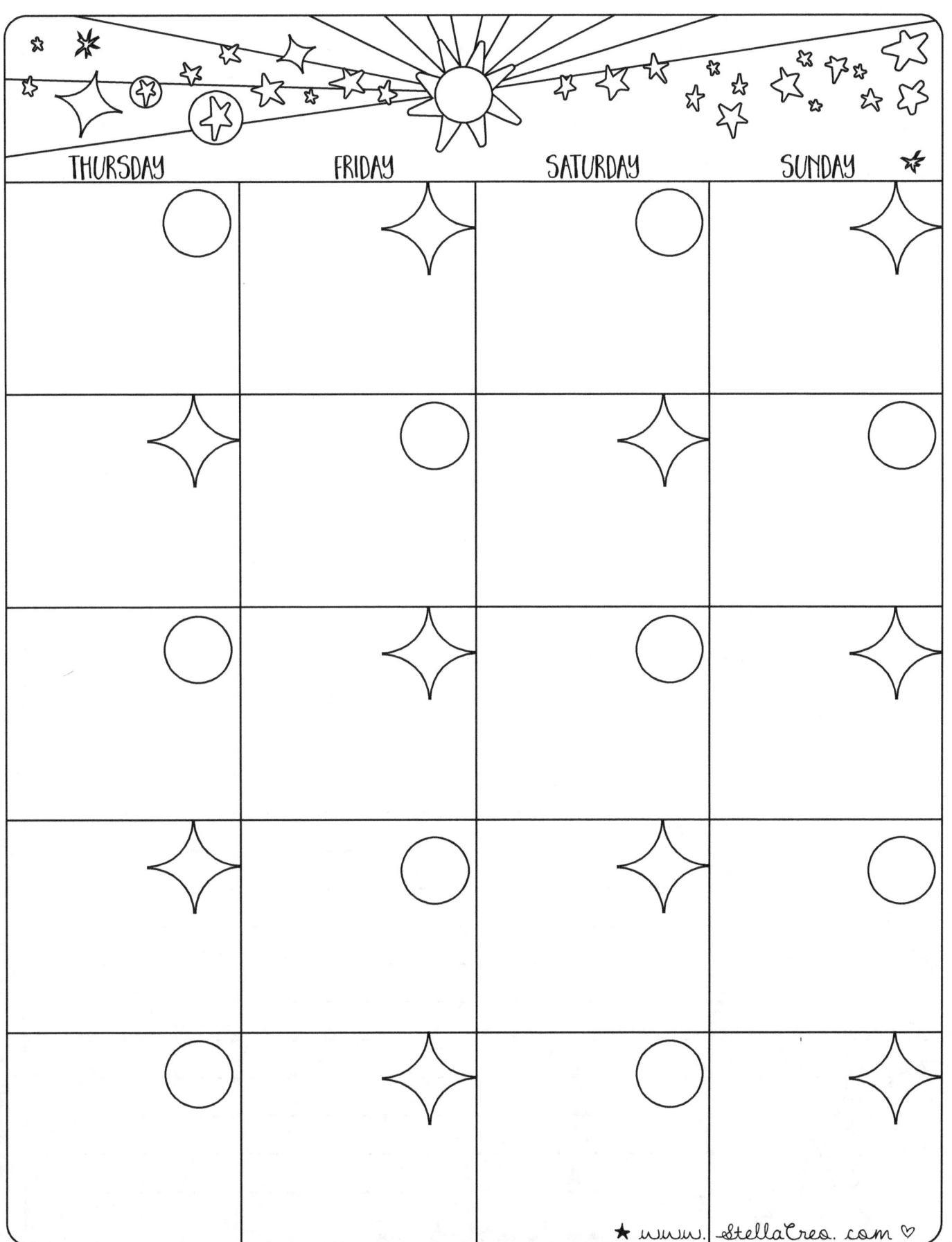

THURSDAY   FRIDAY   SATURDAY   SUNDAY

★ www. stellacrea. com ♡

Notes / Doodles / Dreams
Date:

Month:

MONDAY	TUESDAY	WEDNESDAY
○	☆	○
☆	○	☆
○	☆	○
☆	○	☆
○	☆	○

Want To Do:

Need To Do:

THURSDAY	FRIDAY	SATURDAY	SUNDAY
☆	◯	☆	◯
◯	☆	◯	☆
☆	◯	☆	◯
◯	☆	◯	☆
☆	◯	☆	◯

Notes / Doodles / Dreams
Date:

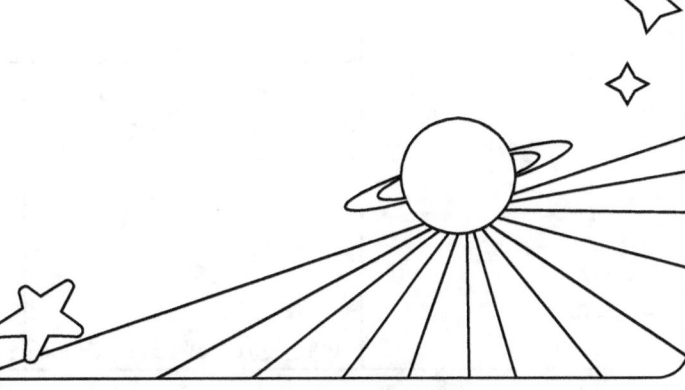

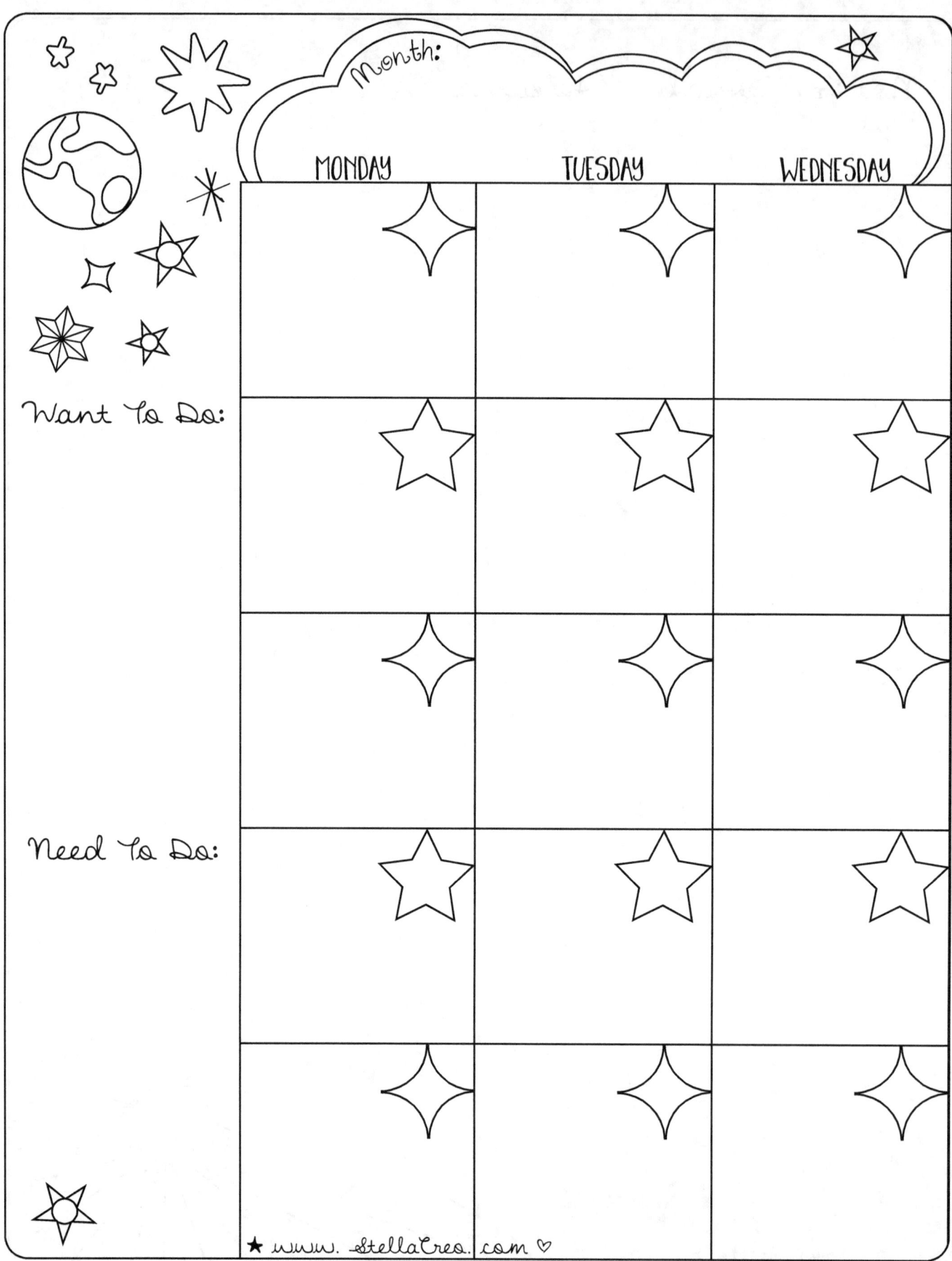

Month:

MONDAY	TUESDAY	WEDNESDAY

Want To Do:

Need To Do:

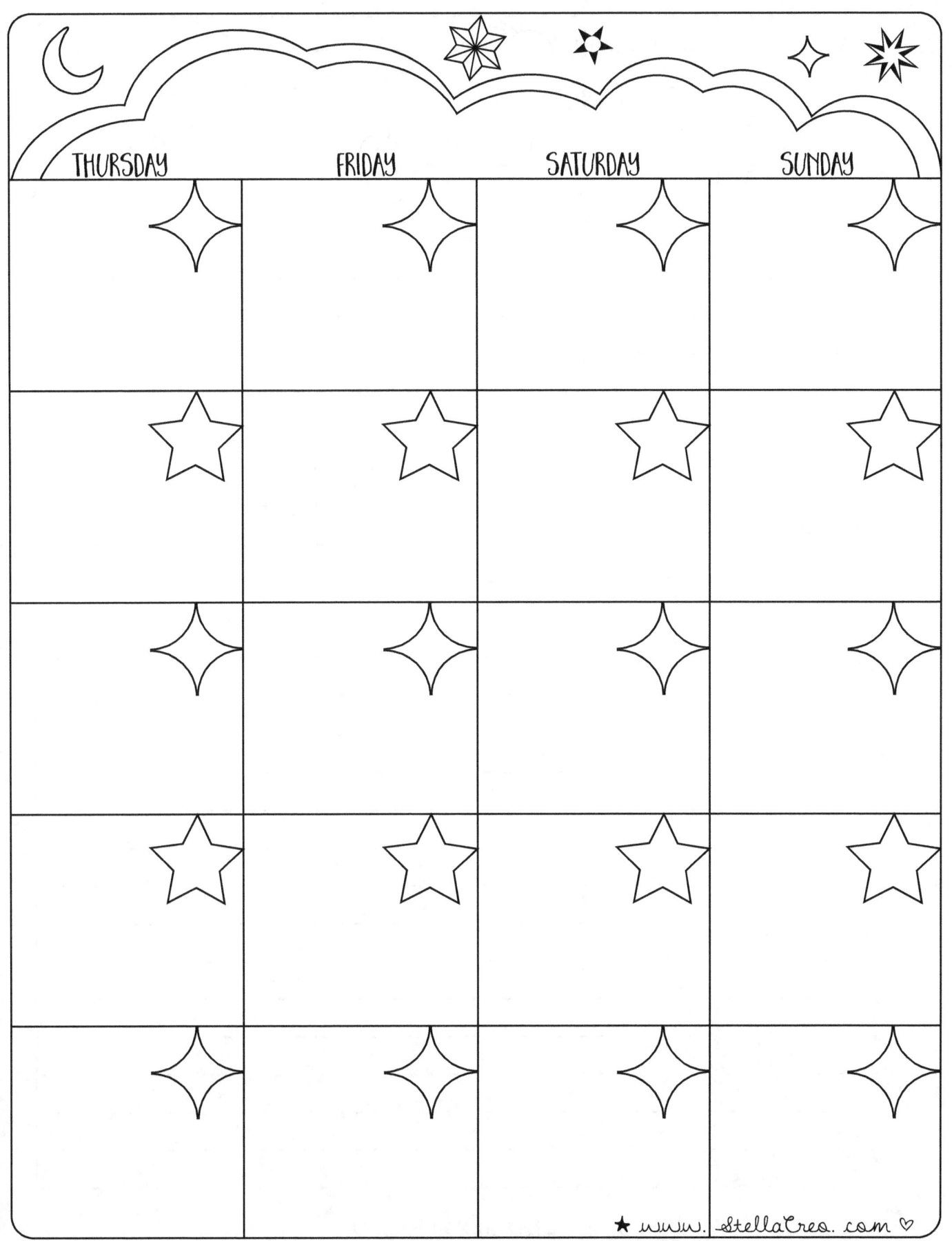

THURSDAY | FRIDAY | SATURDAY | SUNDAY

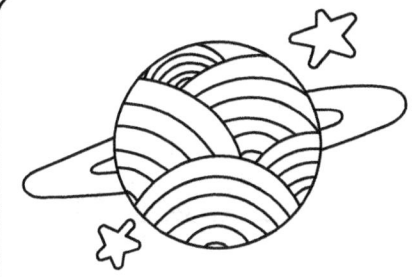

Notes / Doodles / Dreams
Date:

Month:

MONDAY	TUESDAY	WEDNESDAY

Want To Do:

Need To Do:

THURSDAY	FRIDAY	SATURDAY	SUNDAY

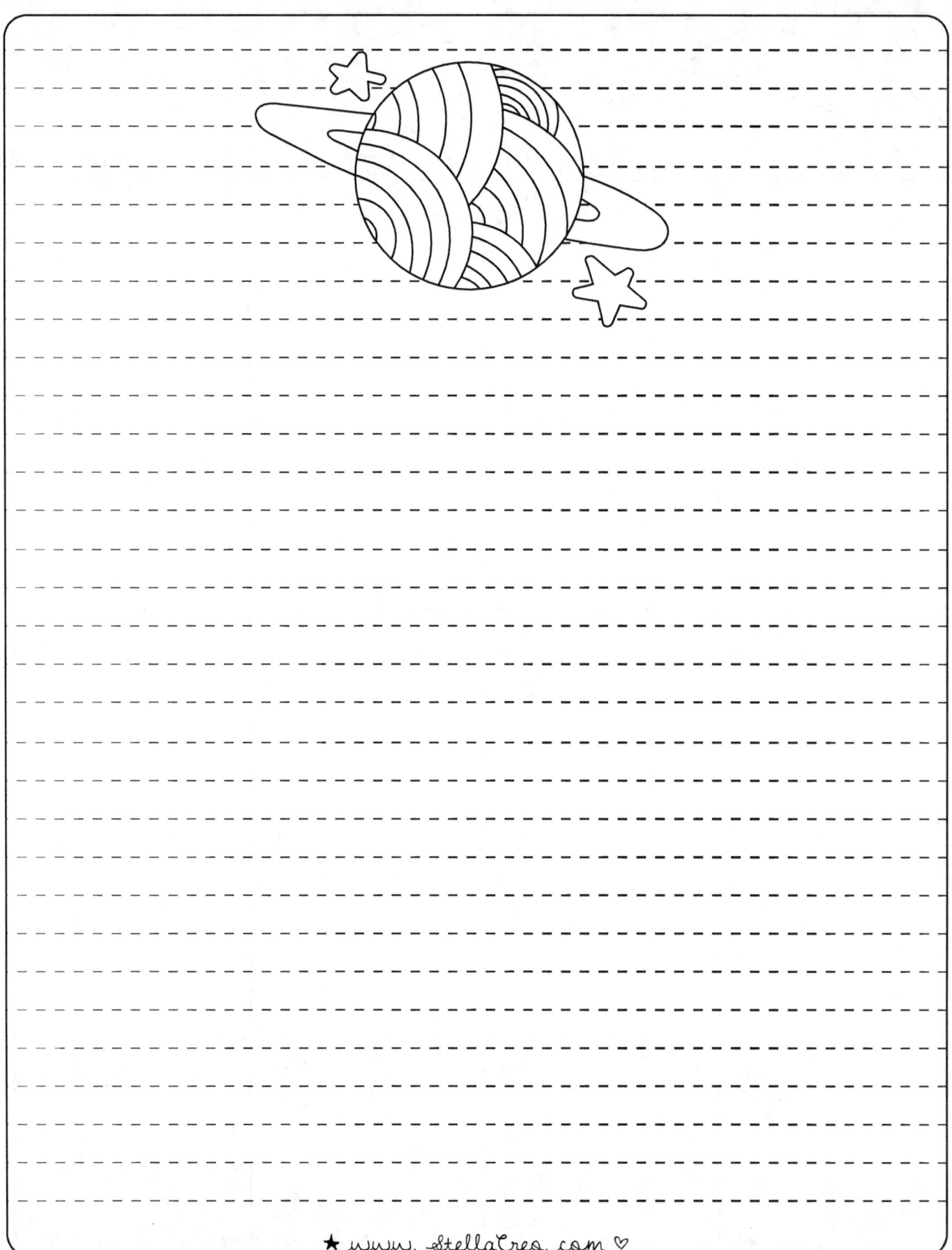

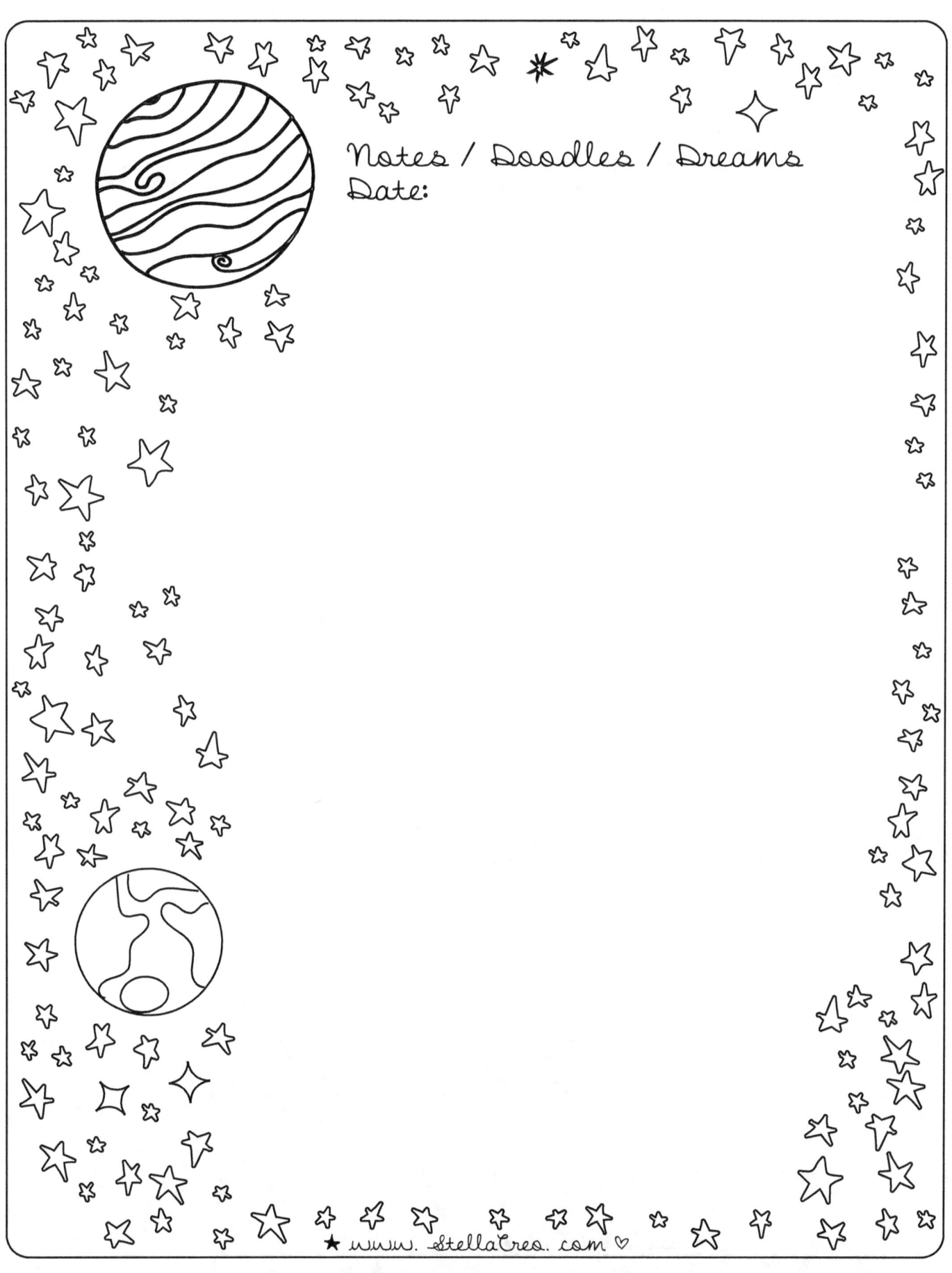

Notes / Doodles / Dreams
Date:

Month:

	MONDAY	TUESDAY	WEDNESDAY

Want To Do:

Need To Do:

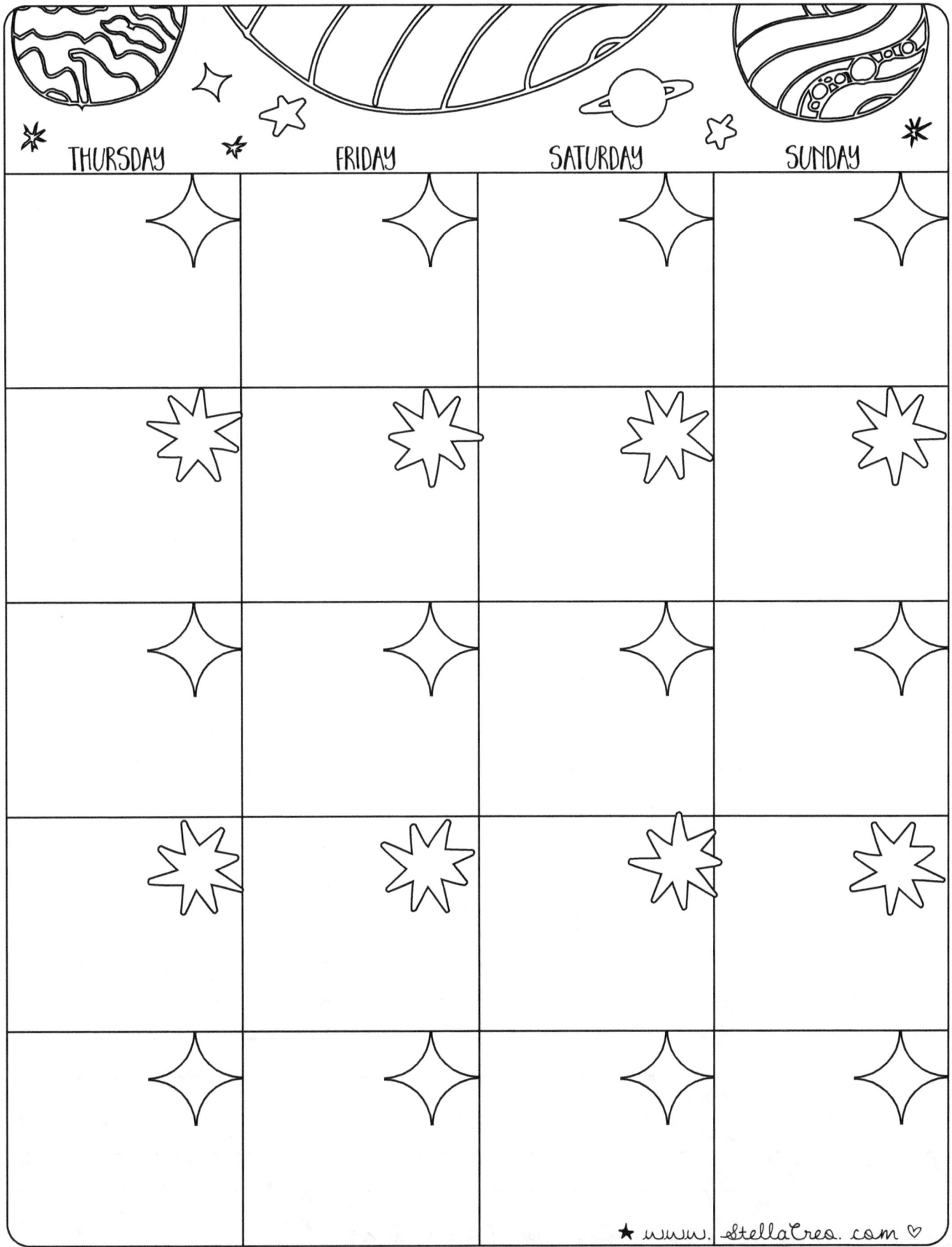

THURSDAY FRIDAY SATURDAY SUNDAY

Notes / Doodles / Dreams
Date:

Month:

MONDAY	TUESDAY	WEDNESDAY

Want To Do:

Need To Do:

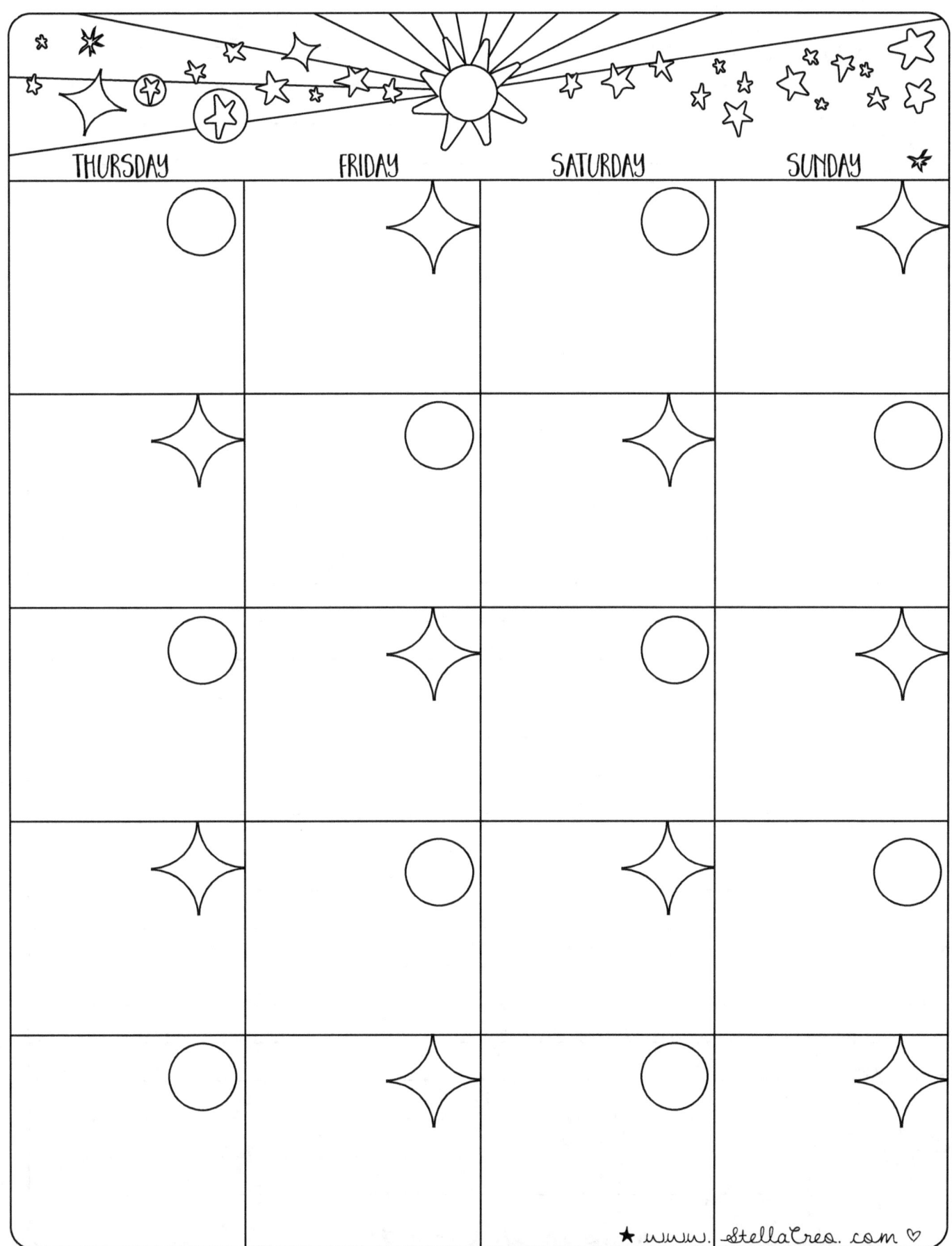

THURSDAY   FRIDAY   SATURDAY   SUNDAY

Notes / Doodles / Dreams
Date:

Month:

MONDAY	TUESDAY	WEDNESDAY
○	★	○
★	○	★
○	★	○
★	○	★
○	★	○

Want To Do:

Need To Do:

★ www.StellaCreo.com ♡

THURSDAY	FRIDAY	SATURDAY	SUNDAY
☆	○	☆	○
○	☆	○	☆
☆	○	☆	○
○	☆	○	☆
☆	○	☆	○

★ www. StellaCrea. com ♡

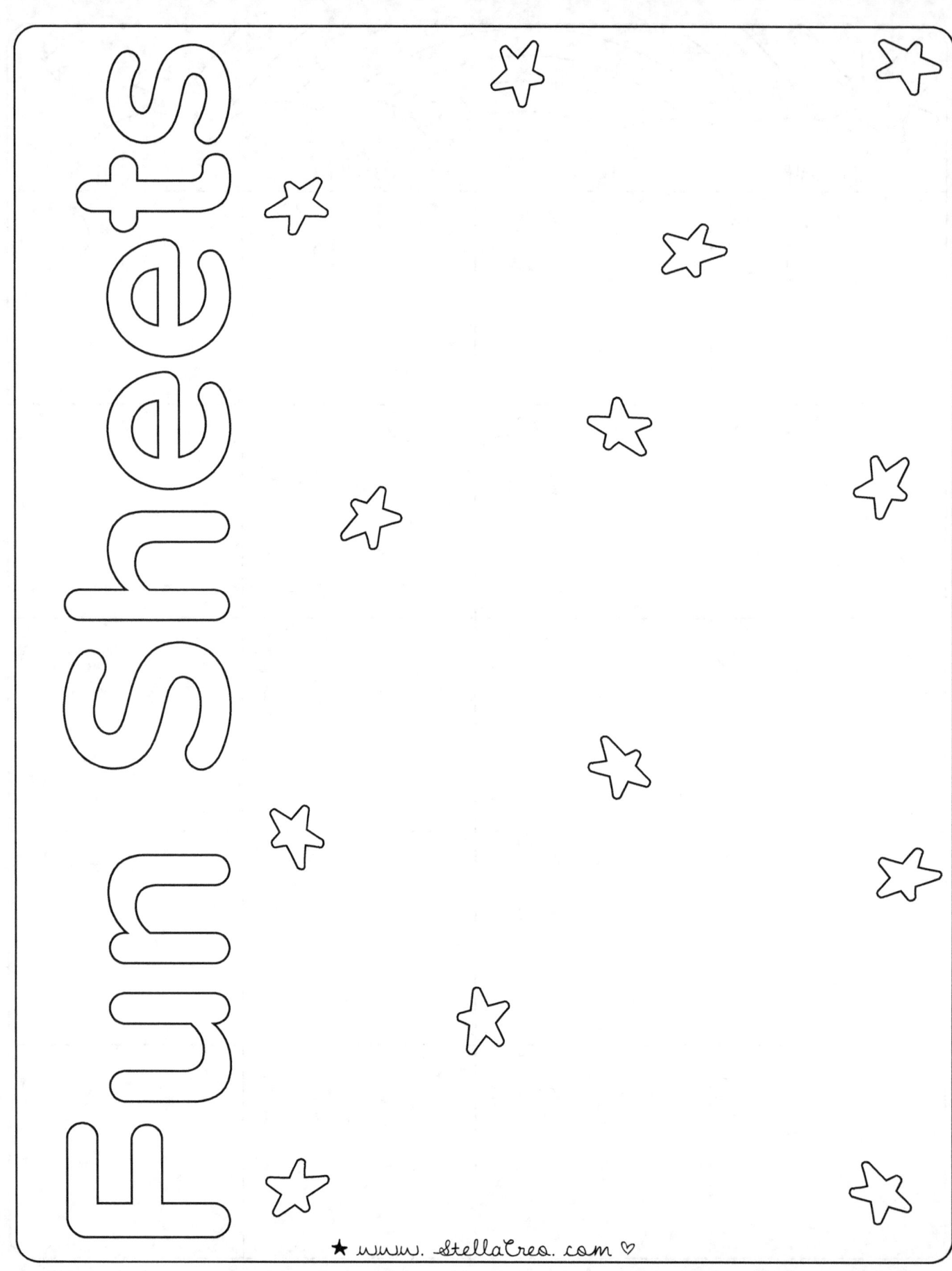

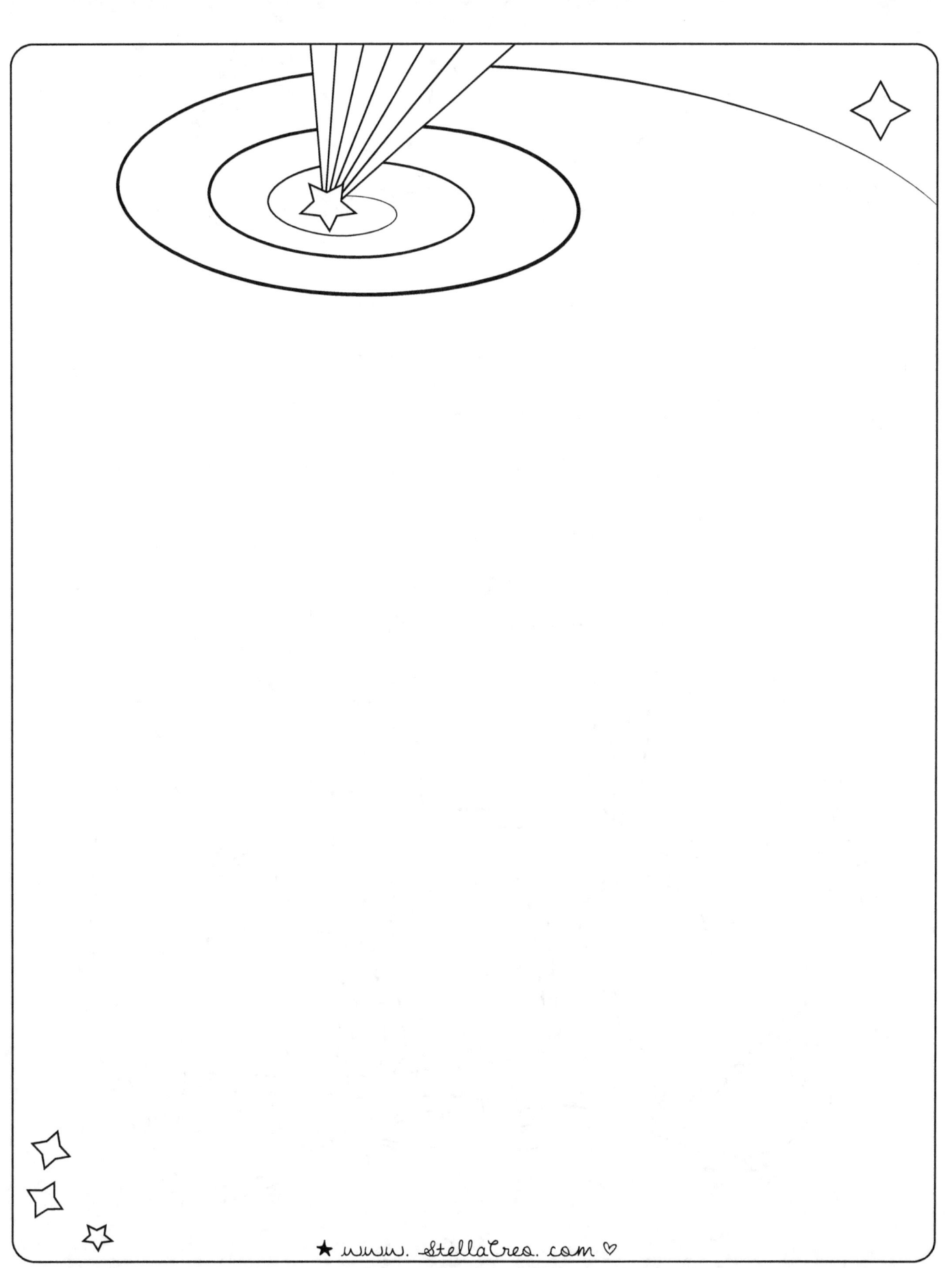

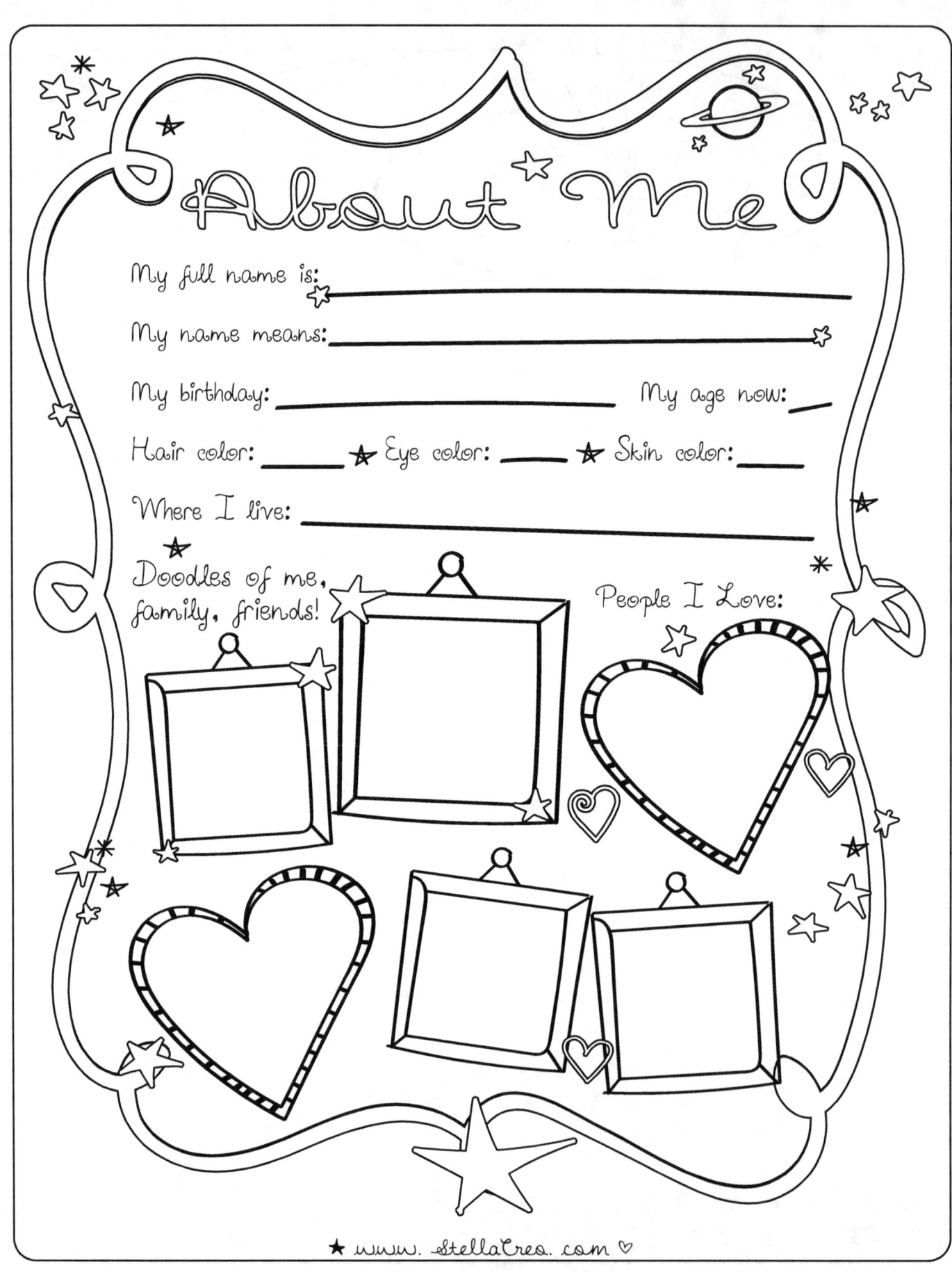

About Me

My full name is: _____

My name means: _____

My birthday: _____ My age now: ___

Hair color: _____ Eye color: _____ Skin color: _____

Where I live: _____

Doodles of me, family, friends!

People I Love:

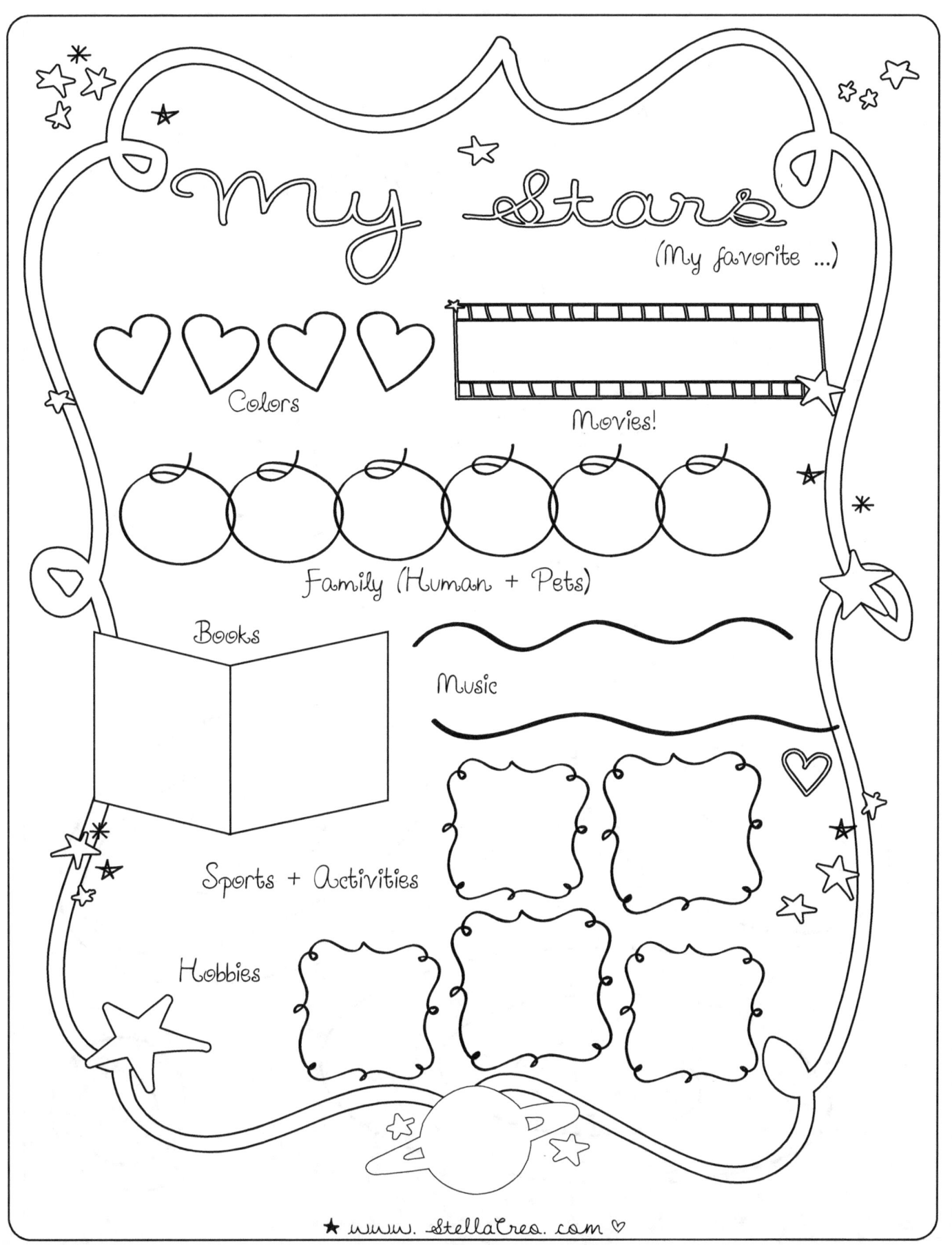

My Stars

(My favorite ...)

Colors

Movies!

Family (Human + Pets)

Books

Music

Sports + Activities

Hobbies

Word Galaxies

To each galaxy, add a few words and/or images that make you happy. Look at this page when you need a pick-me-up. Use your favorite colors and glitter!

Love, Dogs, Stars, Planet, Color, Galaxies

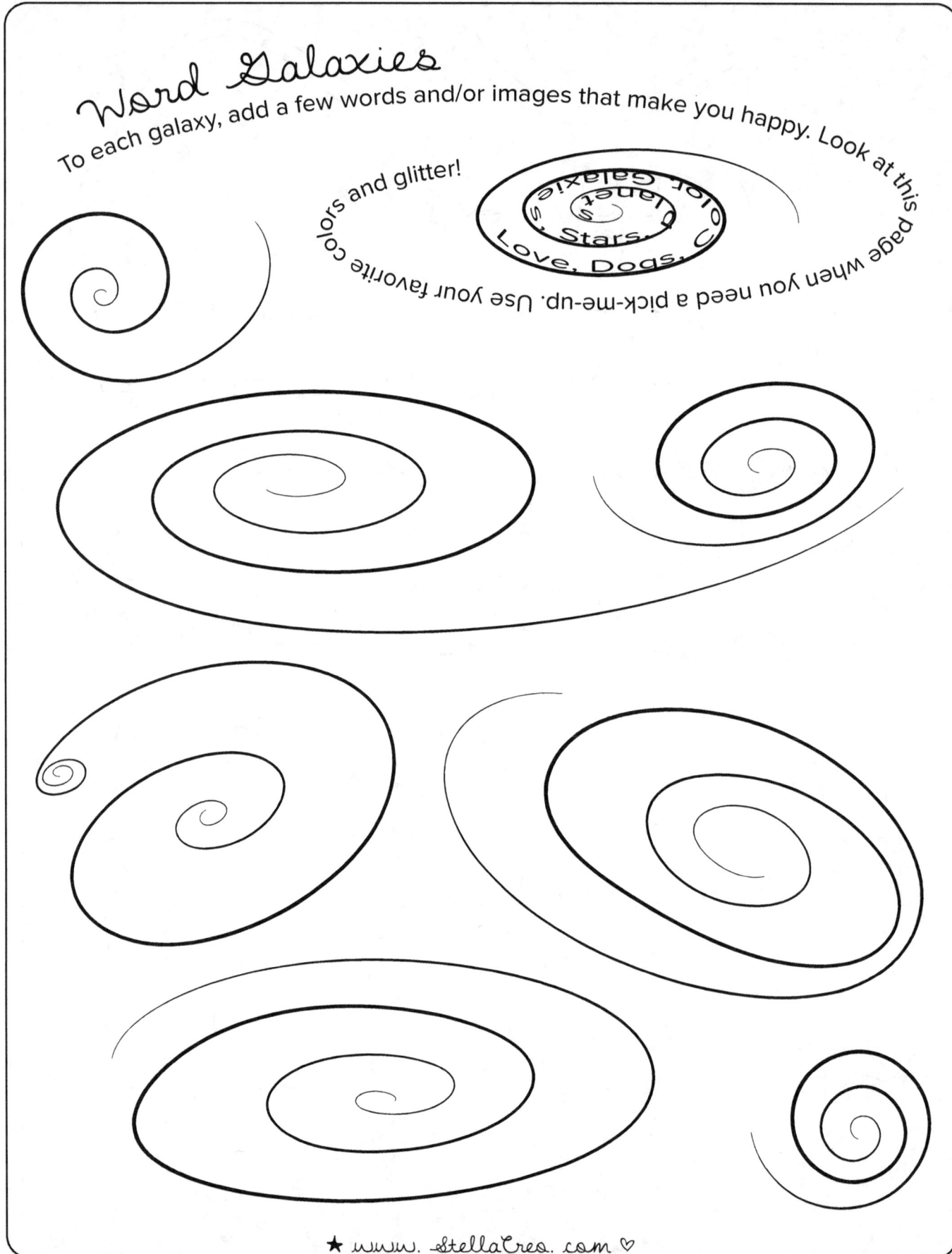

My Universe: What I Love!

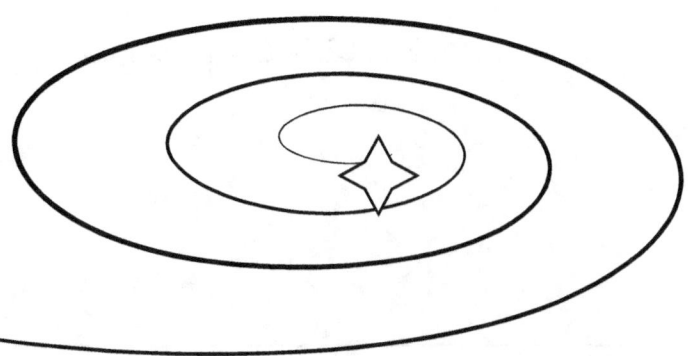

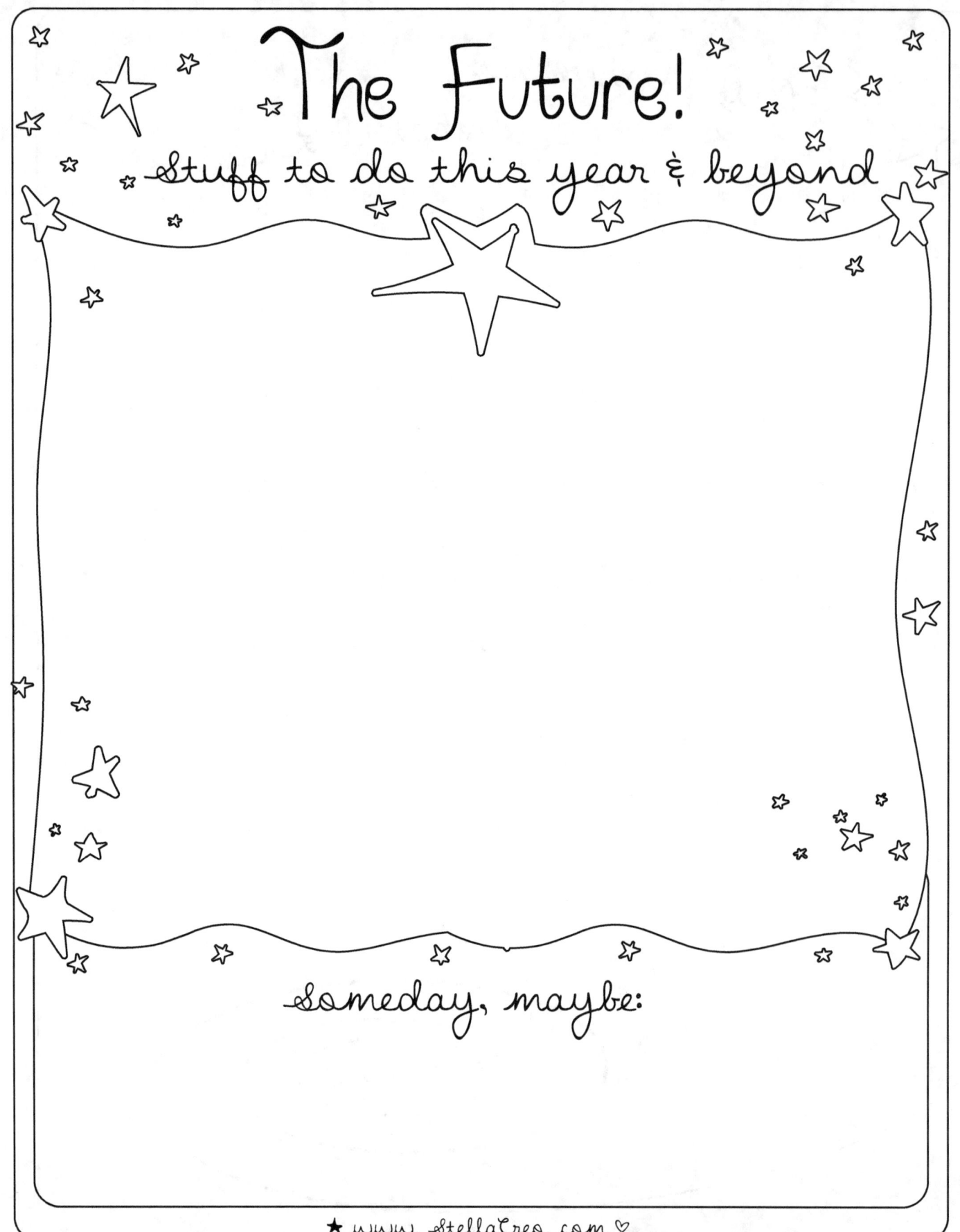

The Future!

Stuff to do this year & beyond

Someday, maybe:

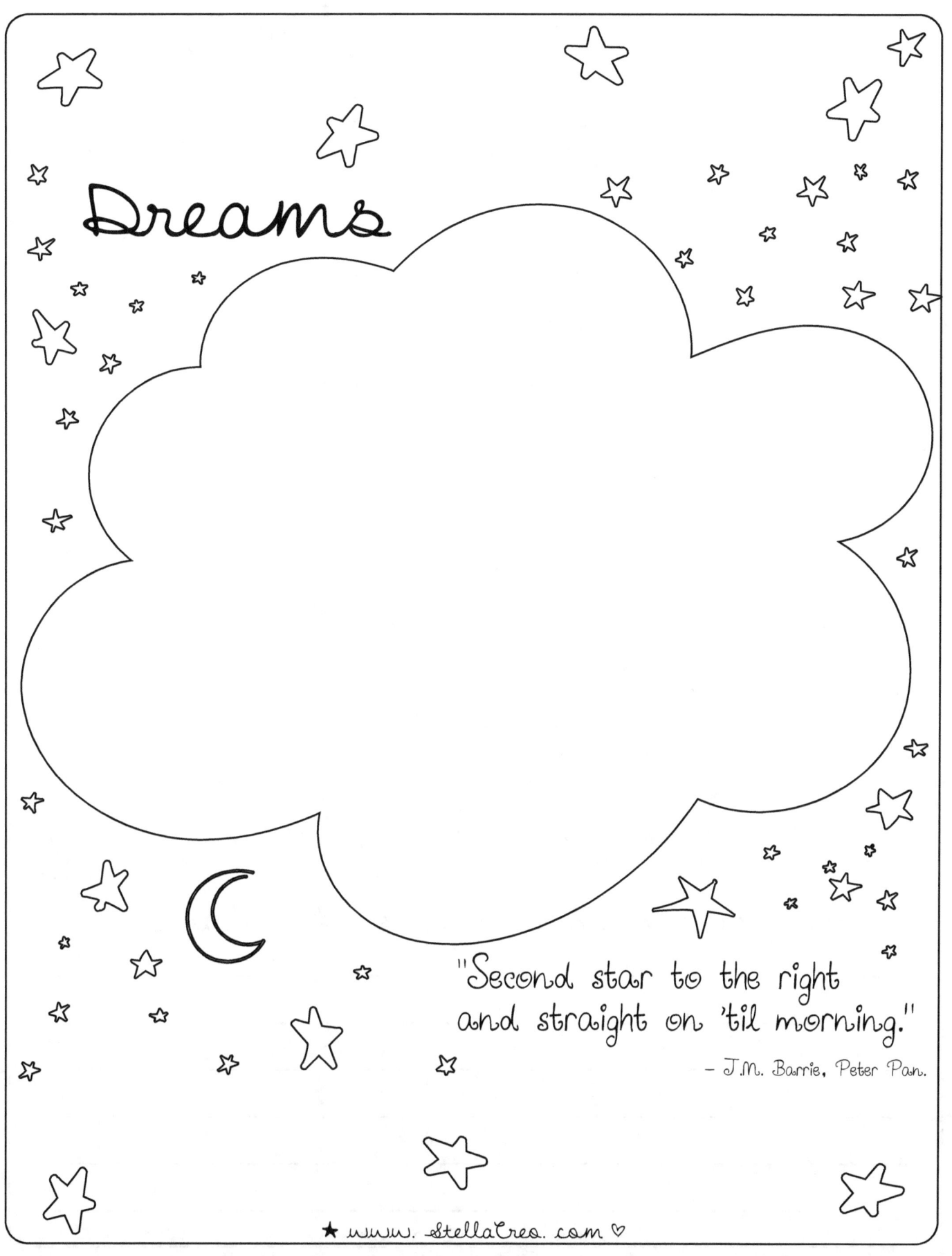

Dreams

"Second star to the right
and straight on 'til morning."

— J.M. Barrie, Peter Pan.

★ www. stellacrea. com ♡

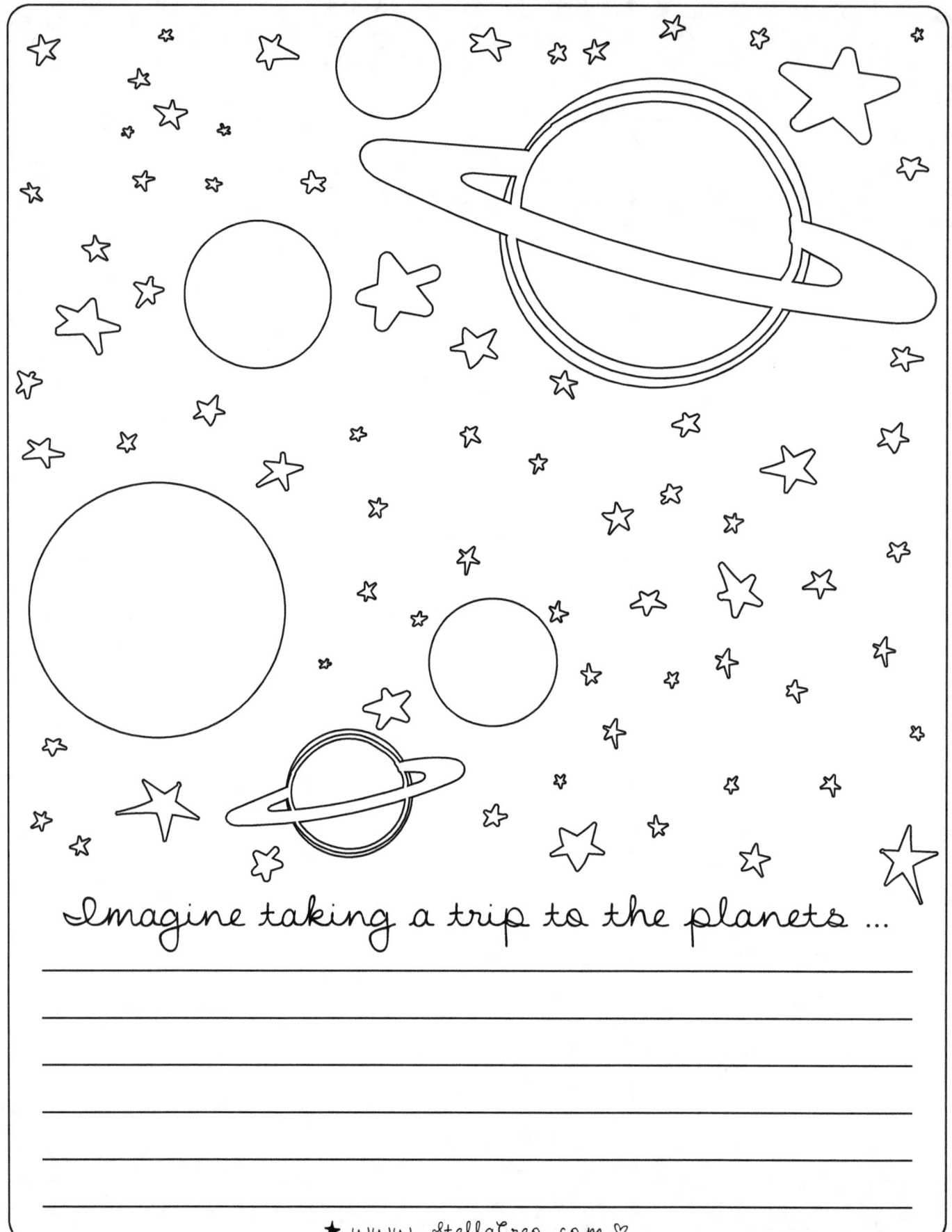

Imagine taking a trip to the planets ...

_____

_____

_____

_____

_____

_____

Planets I Dream of Visiting

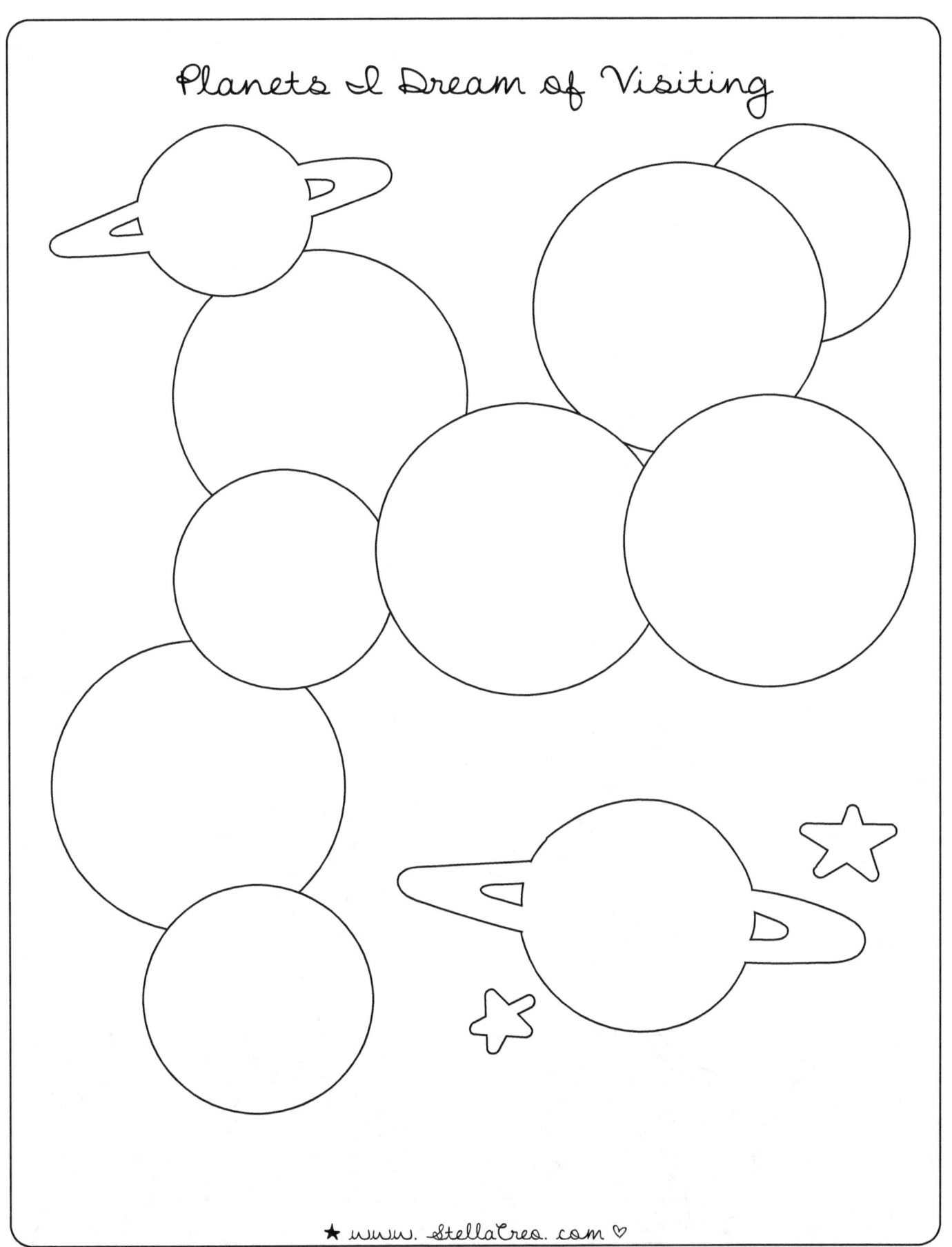

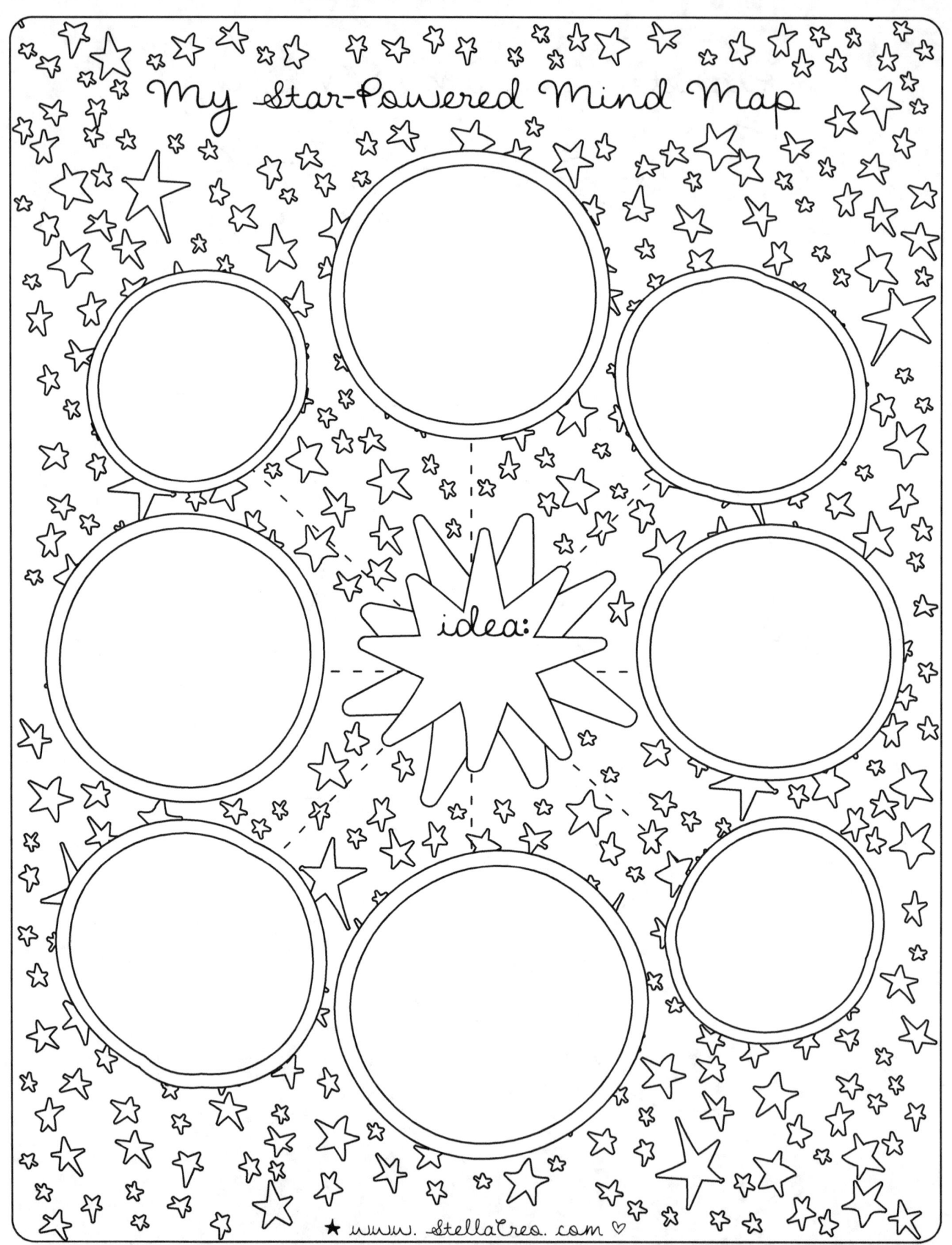

My Star-Powered Mind Map

idea:

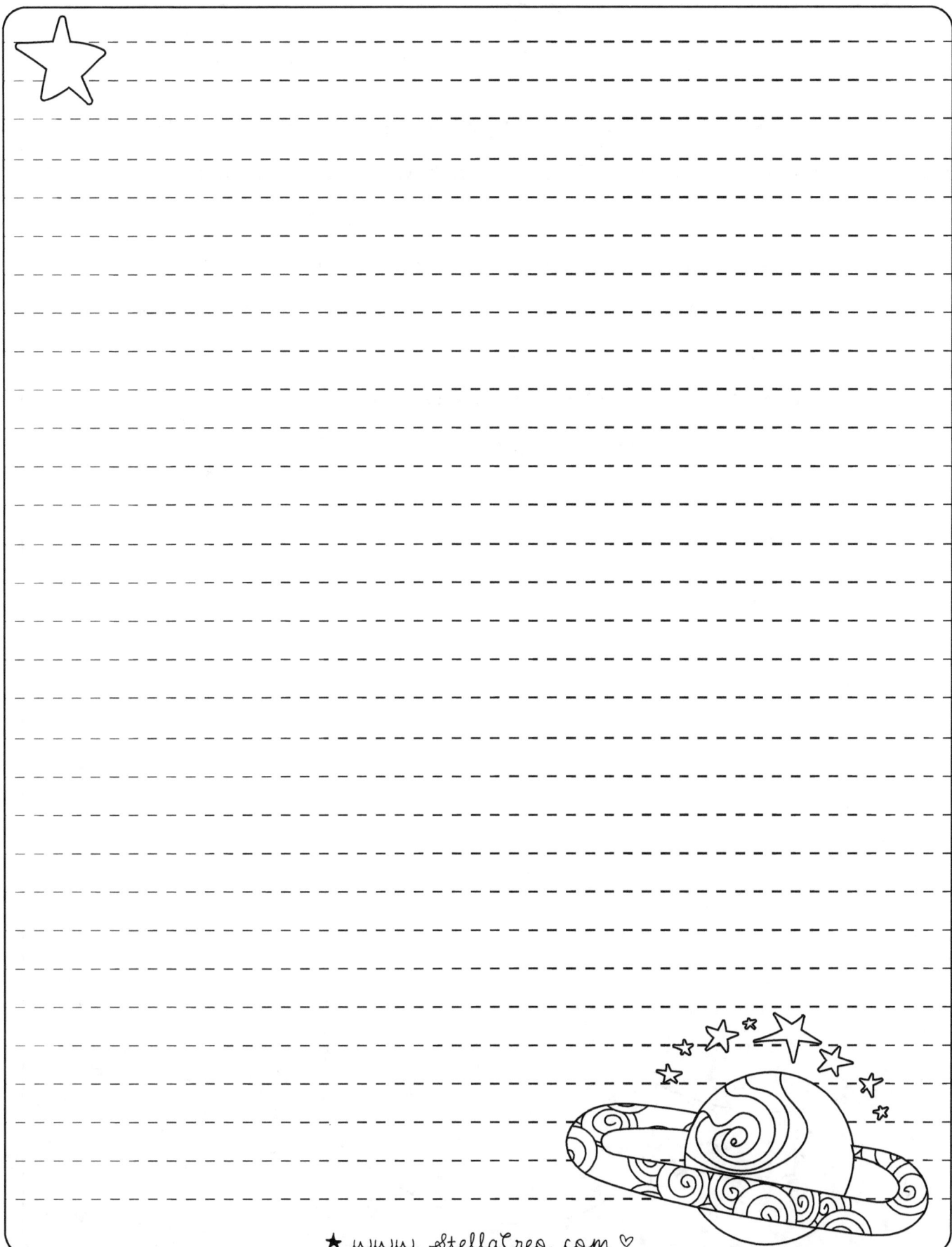

✰ My Big Idea: A Project Planner

Step 1: Capture that spark! Imagine that you've already made your big idea real!

What does it look like? What does it do? What can it help others to do or feel?

Step 2: Gather your ideas in the cloud below. Using your favorite colors, write/draw

anything that comes to mind, especially if it seems crazy or impossible.

Step 3: Organize similar thoughts into groups inside the little clouds and planets. ✰

Step 4: What do you need? Make a list.

Step 5: Make a plan. Step by step. What needs to be done first?

Step 6: Go make it real! Create!

write-draw-doodle

Brainstorm

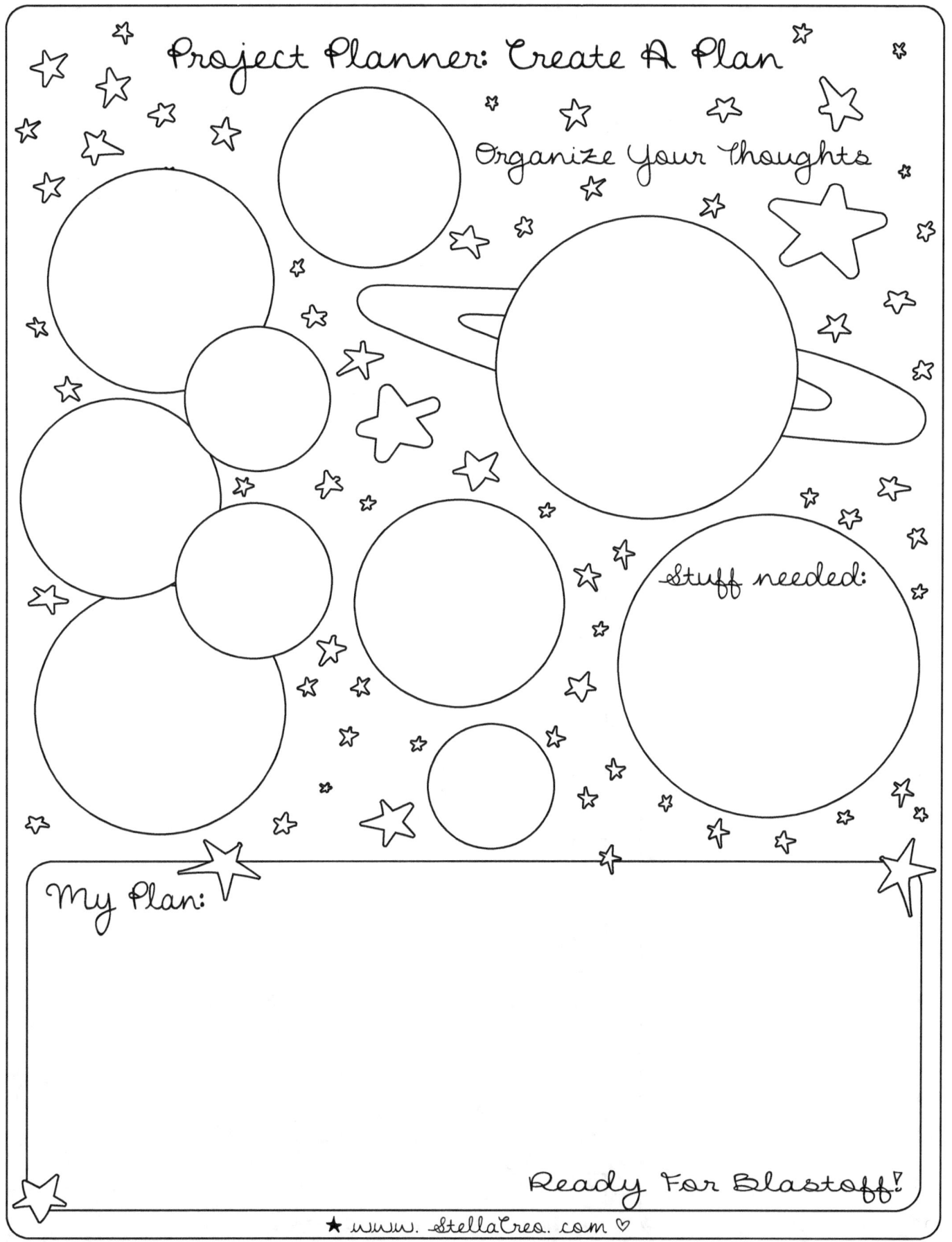

Project Planner: Create A Plan

Organize Your Thoughts

Stuff needed:

My Plan:

Ready For Blastoff!

★ www. stellacrea. com ♡

List:

- [ ] . . . .
- [ ] . . . .
- [ ] . . . .
- [ ] . . . .
- [ ] . . . .
- [ ] . . . .
- [ ] . . . .
- [ ] . . . .
- [ ] . . . .
- [ ] . . . .
- [ ] . . . .
- [ ] . . . .
- [ ] . . . .

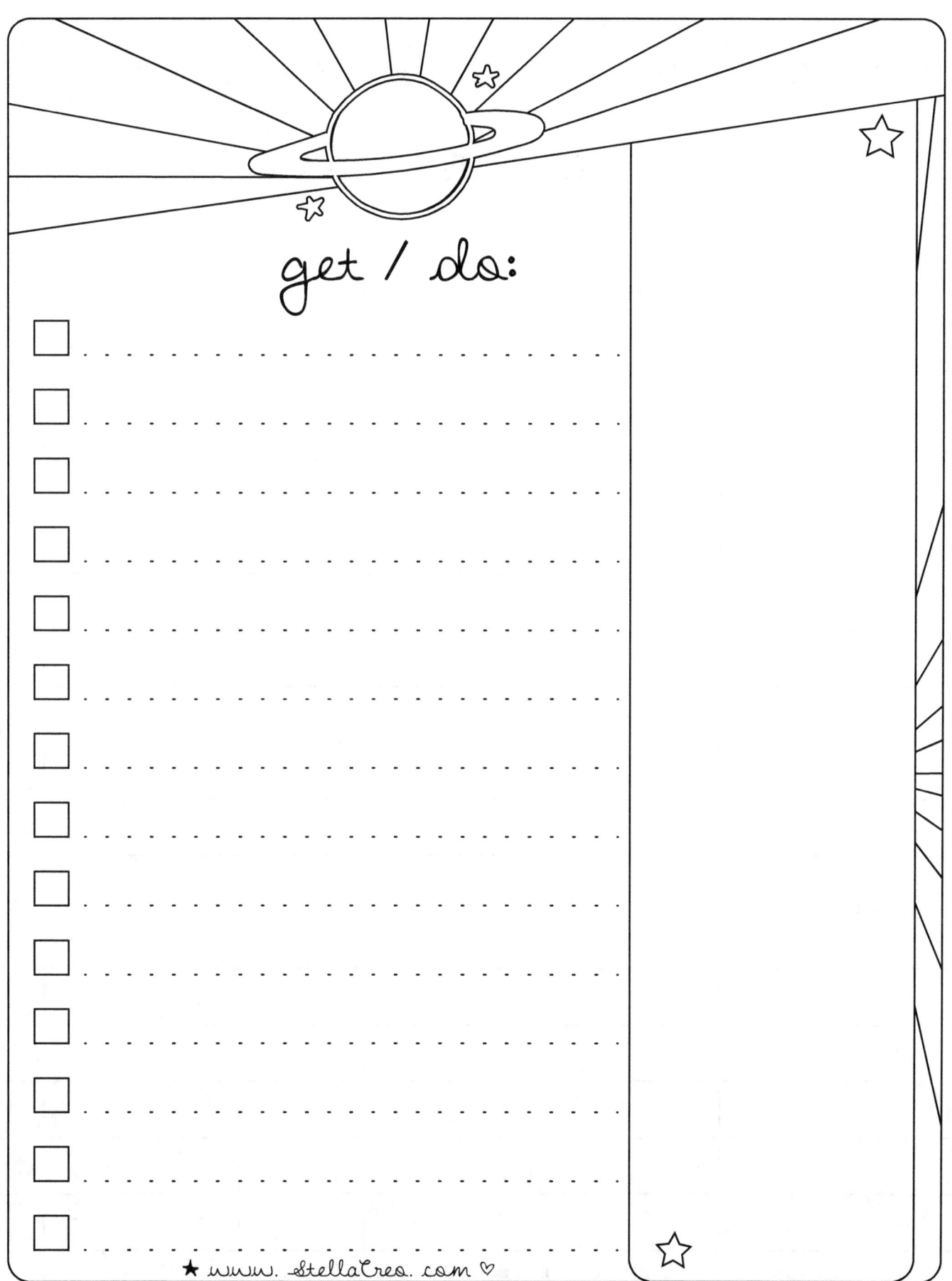

get / do:

- [ ] . . . .
- [ ] . . . .
- [ ] . . . .
- [ ] . . . .
- [ ] . . . .
- [ ] . . . .
- [ ] . . . .
- [ ] . . . .
- [ ] . . . .
- [ ] . . . .
- [ ] . . . .
- [ ] . . . .
- [ ] . . . .

Gift Giving Planner & Checklist

Name	Gift/Idea & Occasion	Cost	Date Given	
				☐
				☆
				☐
				☆
				☐
				☆
				☐
				☆
				☐
				☆
				☐
				☆
				☐
				☆
				☐
				☆
				☐
				☆
				☐

Gifts Received

From	Gift & Occasion	Thanks Given (& Date)	
			☐
			☆
			☐
			☆
			☐
			☆
			☐
			☆
			☐
			☆
			☐
			☆
			☐
			☆
			☐
			☆
			☐
			☆
			★

Stickers for your calendar:

Suggestion: Photocopy to sticker paper. Color. Cut. Stick. Enjoy!

WEEKEND

WEEKEND

Bookmarks

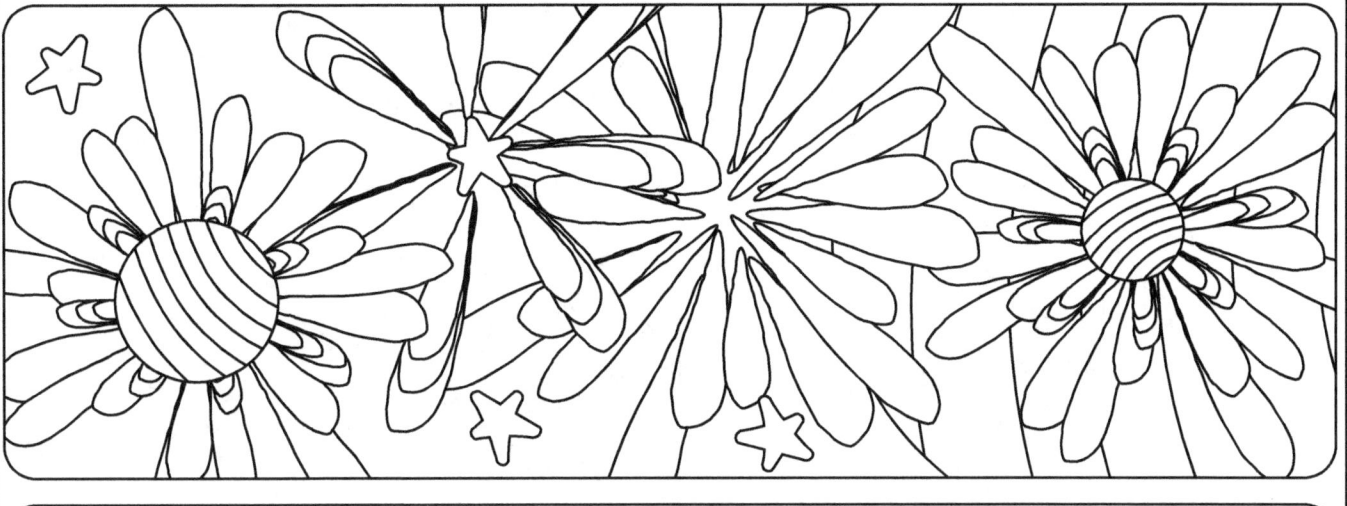

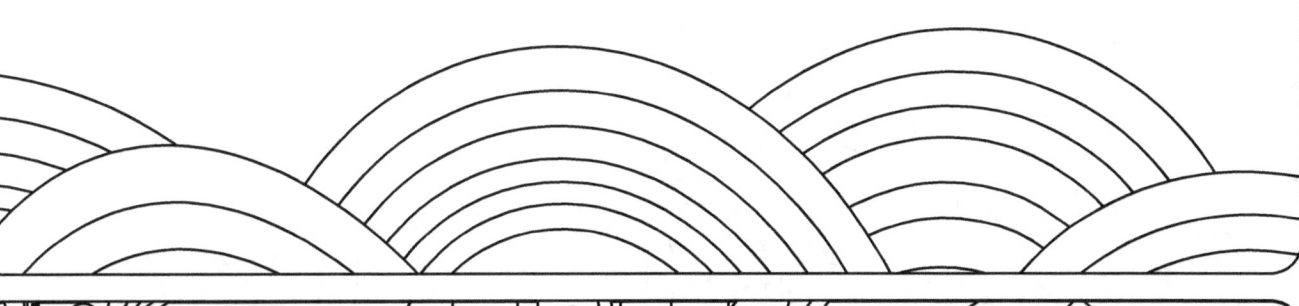

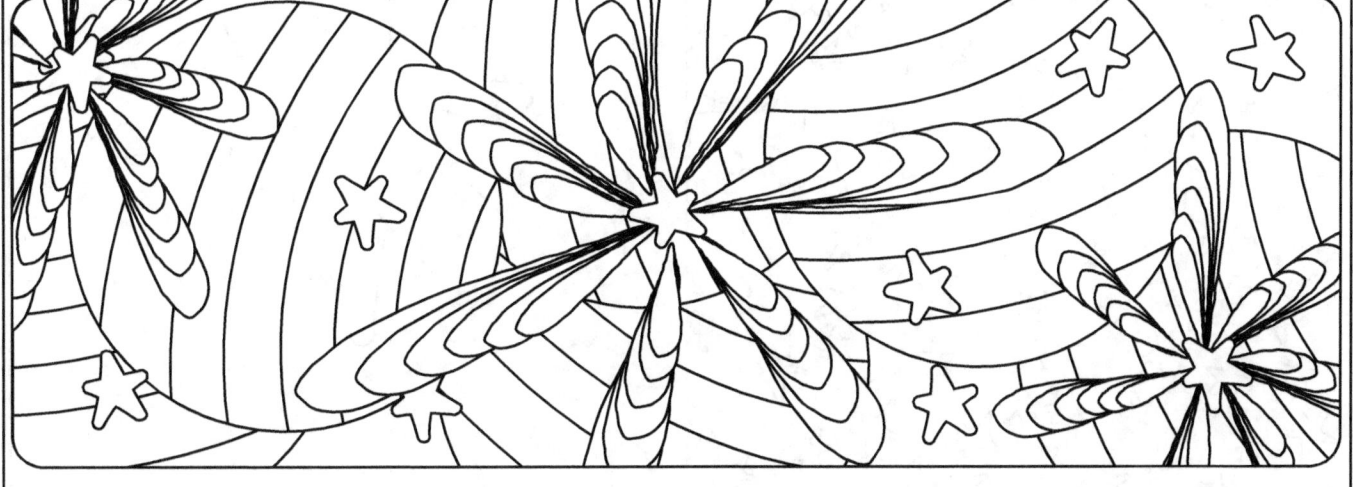

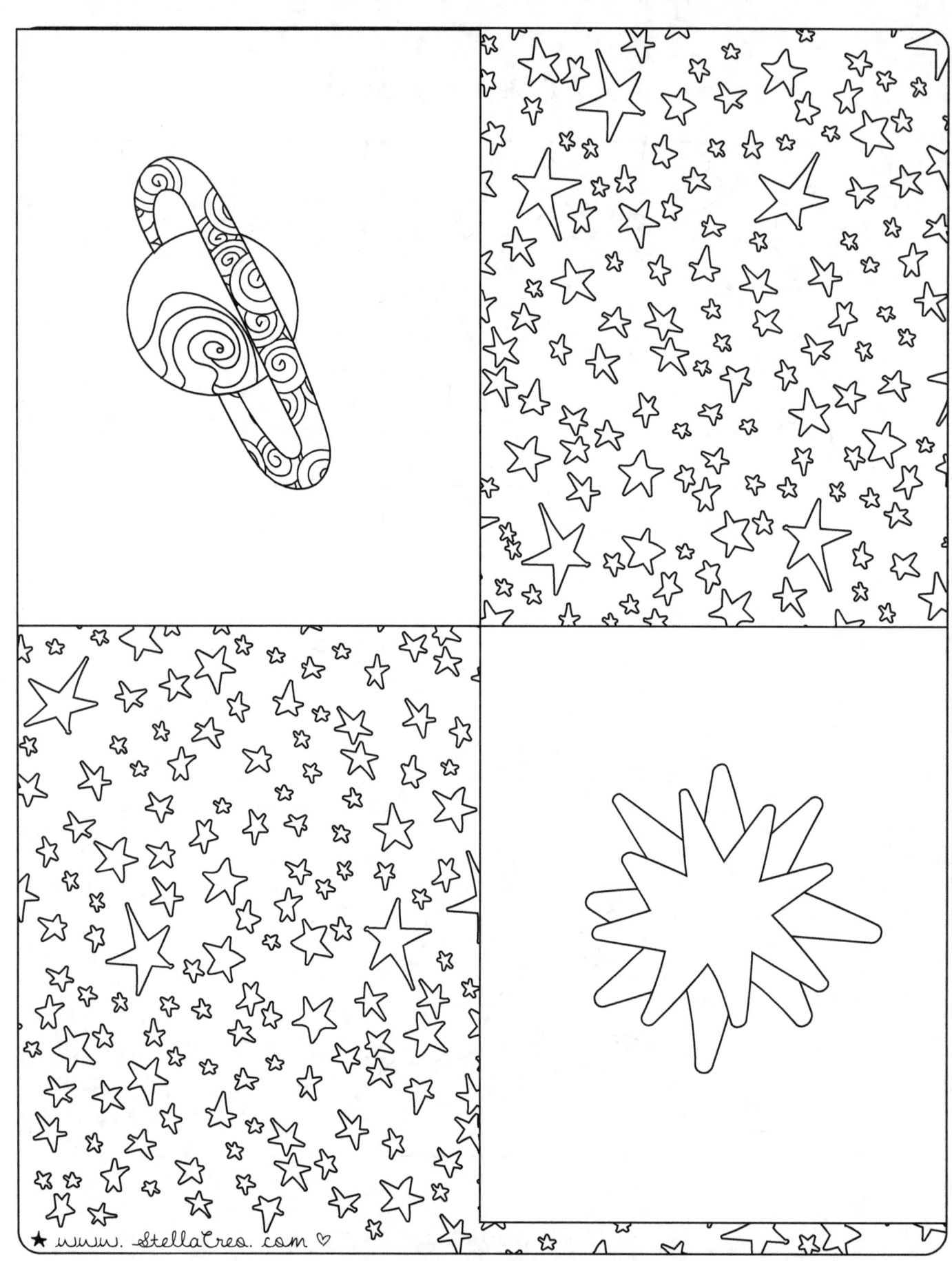

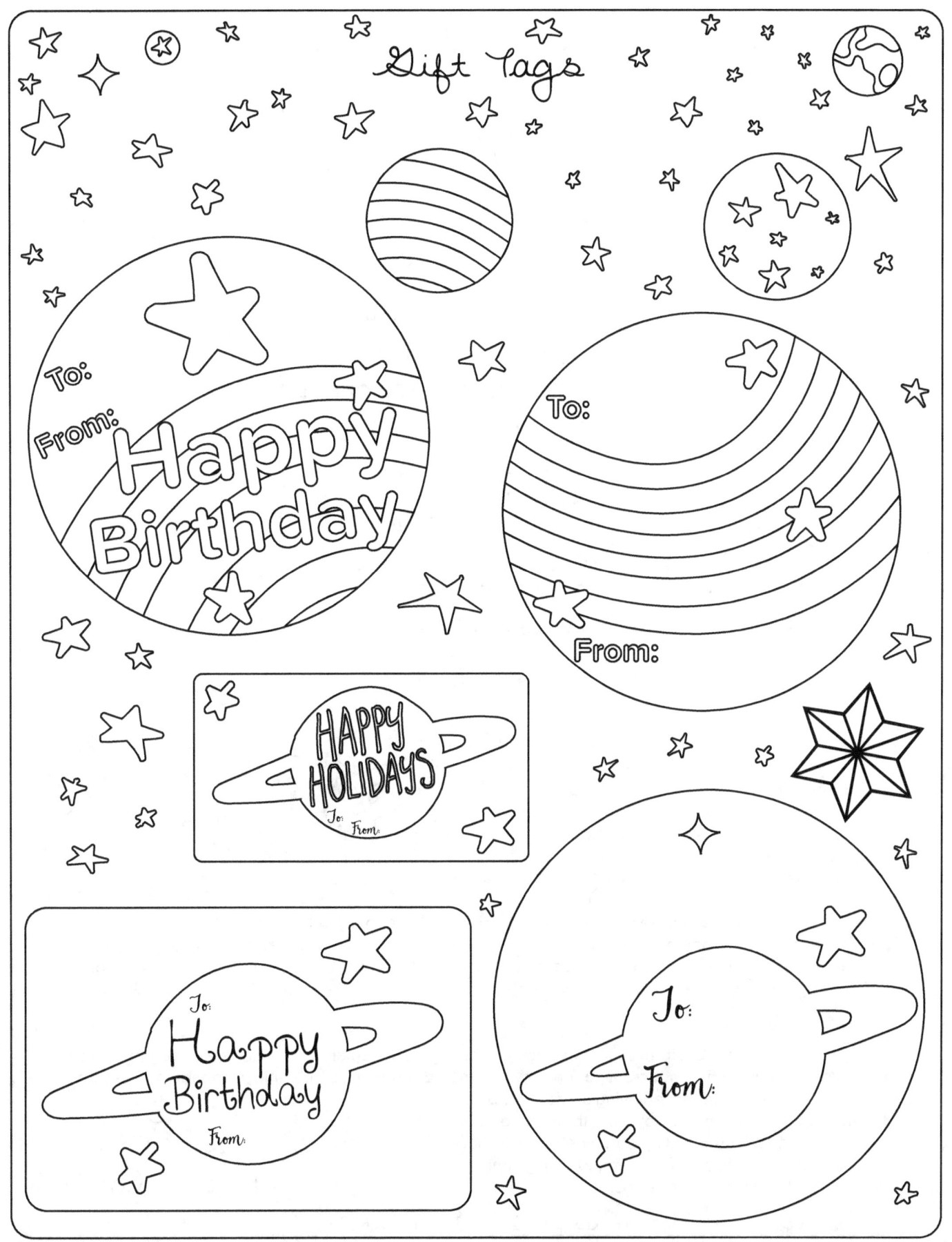

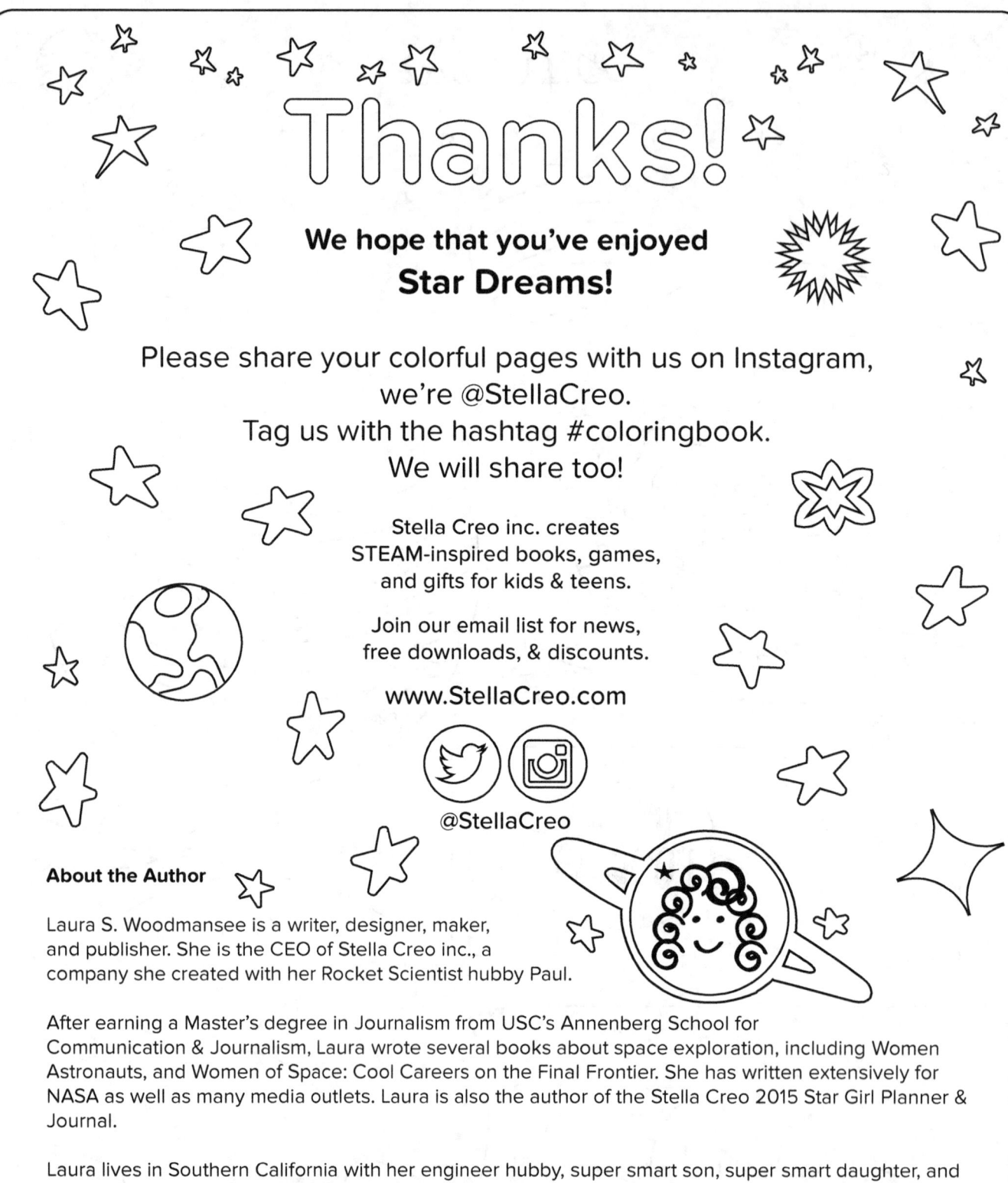

Thanks!

**We hope that you've enjoyed
Star Dreams!**

Please share your colorful pages with us on Instagram,
we're @StellaCreo.
Tag us with the hashtag #coloringbook.
We will share too!

Stella Creo inc. creates
STEAM-inspired books, games,
and gifts for kids & teens.

Join our email list for news,
free downloads, & discounts.

www.StellaCreo.com

@StellaCreo

About the Author

Laura S. Woodmansee is a writer, designer, maker,
and publisher. She is the CEO of Stella Creo inc., a
company she created with her Rocket Scientist hubby Paul.

After earning a Master's degree in Journalism from USC's Annenberg School for
Communication & Journalism, Laura wrote several books about space exploration, including Women
Astronauts, and Women of Space: Cool Careers on the Final Frontier. She has written extensively for
NASA as well as many media outlets. Laura is also the author of the Stella Creo 2015 Star Girl Planner &
Journal.

Laura lives in Southern California with her engineer hubby, super smart son, super smart daughter, and
alien-like dog. When she's not creating fun new books and products, Laura enjoys spending time with
her family, reading, learning, enjoying sci-fi, stargazing, and
dreaming about what (and who) is out there beyond Earth.
In case you haven't guessed by now, she's a true space geek ;)
Keep in touch with Laura on Twitter and Instagram:
@LauraWoodmansee and @StellaCreo.

★ www. StellaCreo. com ♡

www.ingramcontent.com/pod-product-compliance
Lightning Source LLC
Chambersburg PA
CBHW080818170526
45158CB00009B/2465